Light to Live By

how to interpret the Bible

Light to Live By

how to interpret the Bible

Richard Briggs

Scripture Union, 207–209 Queensway, Bletchley, MK2 2EB, England, UK
Email: info@scriptureunion.org.uk
Website: www.scriptureunion.org.uk

Scripture Union Australia
Locked Bag 2, Central Coast Business Centre, NSW 2252
www.su.org.au

British Library Cataloguing-in-Publication data
A catalogue record for this book is available from the British Library.

Cover design: James Kessell
Printed in Great Britain by Creative Book and Design, (Wales) Ebbw Vale

↪ Scripture Union is an international Christian charity working with churches in
more than 130 countries, providing resources to bring the good news about Jesus
Christ to children, young people and families and to encourage them to develop
spiritually through the Bible and prayer.
As well as our network of volunteers, staff and associates who run holidays,
church-based events and school Christian groups, we produce a wide range of
publications and support those who use our resources through training
programmes.

CONTENTS

ACKNOWLEDGEMENTS

The main part of this book (chapters 1–6) was originally written in 1998 and published that year by Scripture Union as *Be an Expert . . . in 137 minutes . . . in Interpreting the Bible*. The series for which that book was written never transpired, and so it is a pleasure to offer it again in this new format. The changes to the revised chapters are minimal: a little smoothing of style, an occasional rethinking of a particularly bad joke, one or two better (and often more straightforward) examples. I was pleased to discover on rereading that I was in considerable agreement with the original author. The introduction is new, as is the survey of Bible translations, and the (new) concluding chapter explores some ideas which are discussed in a different form in my booklet on *Gender and the New Testament* (Grove Books, Cambridge, 2001). Further resources for the task of interpreting what the Bible says about men and women are discussed and references given in that booklet.

I would like to thank Andrew Clark at SU for helping see the book through this revision, and Richard Harvey, companion along the way at All Nations Christian College, for refusing to agree with me on anything but encouraging me with everything. Joshua, Kristin and Matthew have been suitably unimpressed with 'not another book!?' It is a pleasure to dedicate this one to Kristin, even though she really wanted a joke book with her name in it, and is not yet old enough to believe that there might be jokes in a Christian book. Finally, and as always, deepest thanks to Melody, who several years ago was the first person to teach me hermeneutics. I was so impressed that I married her.

To Kristin
who has helped me to see
that wisdom and laughter can go together

DEFINITIONS

hermeneutics (n. pl.)
1. An impressive word for 'interpretation'.
2. A particularly impressive word for 'biblical interpretation'.
3. A hopelessly impressive word for 'discussions about the theory of interpretation'.

Hermann Eutics (n. sing.)
1. A German professor specialising in making the Bible complicated.

hermeneutical (adj.)
1. To do with interpretation.
2. ... That's quite enough definitions. On with the show.

HERMENEUTICS: THE DEMO VERSION

The first time I ever picked up a Bible for myself and decided to read it, I opened it up at the book of Acts, which a friend had recommended to me because it was, so he said, exciting stuff. And I read:

'In my former book, Theophilus, I wrote about . . .'

I was stumped. What former book? Who wrote Acts? I flicked backwards and forwards through my new Bible, checked the somewhat unhelpful contents page, and felt a sense of despair looming over me. In the end I went and asked my friend about who wrote Acts: 'Luke did', he said. And it was so. And there was evening and there was morning: the first lesson in hermeneutics. Sometimes you need background information to understand what is going on.

The second time I made a go at reading the Bible for myself, I was introduced to the apparently well-known Christian routine of the 'Quiet Time'. The Quiet Time is that period of the day when a Christian sits down for a few minutes and quietly reflects on the fact that they haven't read the Bible for ages. They then open the Bible, read some of it, and pray. This is a fantastic invention: package up the biblical stories in bite-sized chunks to be consumed one every morning, over coffee and before the rush of work, just when your mind is at its sharpest and you feel most like thinking about how to change your life and the whole world around you.

Picture the scene: a moment's peace, and then you turn with

trepidation to the Holy Book and read your assigned portion. 'They rose early in the morning and worshipped before the LORD,' you begin in 1 Samuel 1:19. So far so good, for this is precisely what you have done. On you go: 'then they went back to their house at Ramah. Elkanah knew his wife Hannah, and the LORD remembered her.' Is this a 'does anybody know Hannah?' story? Where was Ramah again?

By the end of the short paragraph set for your meditative moment, the biblical text has pulled you a long long way from anything you can quite relate to the day ahead. Bemused, you close the book and get back to asking God to help you drive safely, get your paperwork done, and not forget to pick up Kurt from the station at 3.45. 'Lord, just as you remembered Hannah, please help me to remember Kurt.'

And there was evening and there was (early) morning: the second lesson in hermeneutics. Taking a short piece of the Bible and trying to apply it to your day may not be the best way to take the Bible seriously.

Is there a better way?

The better way, I have concluded, is to take the detour of thinking about how to interpret the Bible early on in your Bible reading. That's what this little book is about. That's what the idea behind thinking about 'hermeneutics' is. The third time I made a serious attempt to get to grips with the Bible, after a lot of puzzled and muddled adventures rather like the ones described above, I finally came across this term 'hermeneutics'. On a good day, I have learned to find it a tremendous help in reading the Bible. To be fair, there are days when hermeneutics is itself puzzling and muddling. That's something else this book is about: demystifying this often complex subject and showing that the Bible, and studying it, can be entertaining as well as demanding.

The Christian church has always lived with hermeneutics, but it has not always called it that. If we define 'hermeneutics' for now as biblical interpretation we will not go far wrong, although later on we will refine that definition a bit. Hermeneutics has perhaps become something of a jargon word in recent times. Some will be suspicious of why, after all those years of just 'reading the Bible and doing what it says' they should suddenly be expected to enter a whole new arena of ideas and jargon. Others may suspect that hermeneutics is just a way of getting round difficult bits of the Bible which we do not want to put into practice. Meanwhile, some will find hermeneutics exciting: a release perhaps from guilt or fear concerning why they do not do everything the Bible says, or an explanation of some mystery of interpretation which has always puzzled them. The majority of us are probably somewhere between these two positions: occasionally enlightened, occasionally suspicious.

The rest of this introduction is therefore a bit like a computer game demo: it will let us flex our muscles on all the different kinds of issues which will come up later in the book, but it will not let us crash the system entirely. So as you learn mouse-control and menu-option-selection for your hermeneutical experience, let us take a quick run around the features of learning to interpret the Bible.

STOP PRESS
DATELINE: 1150 BC
PLACE: OPHRAH, LAND OF ISRAEL
SUBJECT: SMALL DEMONSTRATION – NOT MANY HURT
Police report just faxed in. Source material for Judges 6 follows:

I was proceeding in an orderly manner through Ophrah past the intersection of East 23rd and Oak Street when I saw the accused, with ten members of his youth group, wielding a baseball bat wrapped in sheepskin and setting about a shop front display of coffee and chocolate products made by the well known multinational NesBaal company. He had a fanatical gleam in his eye and was, I would say, scared witless of being caught.

I remained hidden and observed him destroy the aforementioned products and put in their place a considerable quantity of fair trade coffee jars and a listing of local church service times. They then sang 'Lord, I Lift Your Name on High' six times, quietly so as not to disturb the locals, and were just moving into a time of notices. To be frank, the case had 'religious fruitcake' written all over it.

I apprehended the accused, one Gideon ben Joash, and charged him with breach of the peace and loitering with a youth group after midnight. He pleaded divine intervention, something about a sarcastic angel and some burnt cakes, and I informed him that while it was a free country, and everyone was entitled to their own religious beliefs, even ones as daft as his, he was under arrest.

He appears to believe that religious matters are worth fighting for, and that the truth is worth upsetting people for. I recommend that we send him to England. That will knock it out of him.

Seven Test Cases

Here are seven verses raising seven different kinds of issues. Seven is the perfect number of issues to raise, because seven is a very significant number in the Bible. Why this is so is not obvious: that would be a hermeneutical issue. The point here is to show how hermeneutical thinking is required of us by what we find in the Bible. The issues range from large to small. We are only at the question-raising stage. Answers will turn up gradually as the book progresses. Here we go:

(1) *1 Corinthians 15:29*

'What will those people do who receive baptism on behalf of the dead? If the dead are not raised at all, why are people baptized on their behalf?'

Well, why indeed? Here we have the apostle Paul getting a bit frustrated with the church at Corinth which seems to have missed the obvious point that of course the dead are raised because if they are not then the whole practice of baptising for the dead would be a nonsense. This is a pretty straightforward argument, really, in the context of a chapter which makes many arguments for the bodily resurrection. The hermeneutical question it raises has nothing to do with Paul's point, but rather concerns what Paul meant by 'baptism for the dead'. It is the name of a practice carried out today in the Mormon church, who invest in family tree research precisely because they think it is important to baptise for the dead, which for them means baptising people alive today on behalf of those who died before the Mormon church got going.

The best answer to this question is also the simplest: we do not know what Paul was talking about. (Some people use this argument a bit too often, but here it is fair.) The Mormons might conceivably be right, although there is not much evidence on this one. Paul, and the Corinthians too, knew what he was talking about, which of course is part of the problem, because if he had had to explain himself then we would know more about it. But instead, the verse just sits there, reminding us not to get carried away thinking we are in charge of what the Bible is allowed to say. What do we learn? That becoming a good reader of the Bible does not involve understanding it all or pretending that it does not say some fairly obscure things.

(2) *Genesis 5:27*

'Thus all the days of Methuselah were nine hundred and sixty-nine years; and he died.'

Ever have days when you feel really old? Really, really old? Days when what you are working on seems to have been going on forever? Days when the police officers, teachers, bank staff, checkout staff, and indeed everyone, seem to be getting younger and younger? Is this what it was like for Methuselah? Did he have a good pension plan? Did he invest in companies who made candles for birthday cakes?

These questions, of course, have nothing to do with Genesis 5:27, as we all know. But then what is Genesis 5:27 really saying? Did Methuselah really live to 969 years old? Were they 'earth years' as science fiction writers might say? Did they count differently then or were 'years' really something else (like months? or seasons?). Does it make a difference if we happen to know, as most of us surely do not, that other ancient lists of kings in the beginning of the world's history regularly give their kings ages in the region of 30,000 years? In comparison Methuselah seems like something of a spring chicken. Did the writer of Genesis not know that people do not really live this long? Or is he in fact saying that people *didn't* live to extreme ages like 30,000, but were just ordinary people like you and me, though a little bit special because they lived nearer the earth's life-giving beginning than we do?

If we did not have alternative sources of information about human life span perhaps we would simply take the figure at face value, but the interpretative issues begin when we try to match up this text to what we know either about how long humans live, or how long people were thought to live in the ancient world. Interpreting the Bible might be easier if we never tried to relate it to anything, but the complications are presumably worthwhile.

(3) *1 Corinthians 14:35*

'If there is anything they [women] desire to know, let them ask their husbands at home. For it is shameful for a woman to speak in church.'

Baptism for the dead and the age of Methuselah aside, here is an example which worries us immediately: can we really argue that it is shameful for a woman to speak in church? For half the human race, this one makes a profound difference. (One would hope it would trouble the other half of the human race too . . .) Well, there are several ways people approach this verse. Perhaps Paul did not in fact write this? There is some evidence (though not very much, admittedly) that 1 Corinthians 14:34–36 was added in later after the letter was originally written. If Paul did write it then it is odd that three chapters earlier (see 11:4,5) Paul was patiently explaining how churches should organise men and women who pray and prophesy: he surely did not mean that women would prophesy silently? Some people think there is a cultural issue to do with those women who were uneducated who would distract the church's worship by asking lots of uninformed questions, and they, says Paul, should ask their husbands at home. Clearly this verse does not transfer well into a situation where most women are well-educated and many do not have husbands at home. Others argue that what is at stake here is not just any kind of speaking in church, which is clearly allowed elsewhere in the letter, but is a particular kind of speaking such as the public weighing up of prophecies, which Paul (perhaps) thinks only men should do. Another approach suggests that in this verse Paul is quoting, as he does elsewhere, a saying of the Corinthians which he is about to oppose roundly, when in verse 36 he chides them with, 'Or did the word of God originate with you?' as if to say that verses 34,35 cannot possibly be right. Yet others just throw up their hands in horror and say, 'Well it can't be right, whatever it means.' To them perhaps Paul would say, 'I desire that those should be holy hands . . .' (see 1 Timothy 2:8, just before another much discussed verse about women's silence).

At least five options have been presented already, but of course in a demo program you are unable to access the full analysis. Since this is a hugely important topic, we will in fact return to it in a later chapter where we ask how to go about interpreting the Bible on a particular theme (see chapter 7). For now, one simple observation: even faced with the most challenging and difficult of verses in the Bible, there are usually a large number of different interpretations available rather than just a simple 'yes, I believe it' or 'no, I don't'. Working out what was actually being said is not always straightforward.

(4) *Job 1:8*

'The LORD said to Satan, "Have you considered my servant Job? There is no one like him on the earth."'

Now this is a really encouraging verse, is it not? Ideal for a little quiet meditation first thing in the morning. Who should fear as they behold all that might lie in wait, because no matter what the day holds, the Lord is busy pointing out to Satan those who are doing really well and suggesting that they might be a suitable target for the latter's attentions!

If this does not sound right (and it should not sound right) then what does that tell us about interpretation? How are we to tell if this description of something the Lord wants to do is a one-off or if it might be the sort of thing God would do again?

There is another puzzle in this verse, which will only bother people who read the New Testament as well as the Old Testament. Job is described as 'blameless and upright'. But according to the apostle Paul, there is no one blameless: not even one. (Romans 3:9–20 makes this point rather clearly.) So how many people like Job are there? None. Which may in turn prompt us to reflect on what sort of story the book of Job is telling. It appears to be tackling a variety of issues around the 'how do we make sense of terrible things which happen to us?' area. Are such things God's fault? Is it that we haven't prayed enough? Or confessed enough sin? Is it just the random experience of an impersonal universe? The book begins to seem like an extended exercise in exploring these questions rather than a description of something God actually did to a particular Job.

Well, we may say, why not indicate that then? Why not start the book off in a way that makes it clear that it is a kind of story or fable? What about 'Once upon a time . . .'? We turn to Job 1:1 and read instead: 'There was once a man in the land of Uz whose name was Job . . .' Perhaps that's as near as they got in ancient Hebrew to 'Once upon a time' after all.

(5) *Matthew 5:40*

'If anyone wants to sue you and take your coat, give your cloak as well.'

This verse presents very few difficulties of understanding. 'Coat' means 'coat'. 'Cloak' means 'cloak'. These words of Jesus do not seem to offer much in the way of a get-out clause.

This is one of several sayings from the so-called 'Sermon on the Mount', one of the most famous bits of Christian teaching of all time. But also one of the most difficult to apply to daily living. The hermeneutical issue comes when you try and work out how to live in response to this verse. Is it really suggesting that if you are sued you should simply pay up, indeed pay double, and leave it at that? I once knew a Christian organisation being sued by somebody. It certainly didn't seem the obvious thing that they should pay up, even excepting the point that they had no money anyway.

I have often thought that the Sermon on the Mount is a good passage to read with people who say, 'You don't need to interpret the Bible: just do what it says'. In Luke's version of the sermon we read, 'Love your enemies, do good, and lend, expecting nothing in return' (Luke 6:35). After reading this together, ask them to lend you their car, or laptop, or cash card. And see what sort of hermeneutical reaction suddenly swings into view after all.

(6) *Isaiah 1:18*

'Come now, let us reason together, says the LORD. Though your sins are like scarlet, they shall be as white as snow' (NIV).

One frequent issue in interpreting the Bible is checking that the associations we may have with a particular image or symbol are anything to do with the associations that image would have had when it was originally written. Little children, for instance, in some of Jesus' sayings, are not so much meant to make us think of innocence or sweetness, in a fluffy greeting card kind of way, rather they indicate people who are powerless and have no social status. To become like a little child is not to be sweet and innocent, but to take on powerlessness.

I start with that example, which is not in the verse we are discussing, because the example which is in the verse we are discussing seems harder to shift in a lot of people's thinking. Isaiah 1:18 has typically been used to adorn attractive posters of rural English churches nestling in the snow-covered hills: come to the Lord and let us work our way to whiteness and purity, the poster says. And on the whole, this is how people often read Isaiah 1:18 itself: our sins may be washed away, and we may be washed white as snow, if we turn to the Lord and 'reason' (in other words: confess our sins).

There is nothing wrong with this point, but is it what Isaiah wants to say? Who gets to say what 'white' symbolises in the world of the Old Testament? Is there any reason to think that white is a positive symbol? One clear route open to us is to explore other places where the phrase 'white as snow' is used in the Old Testament and see what it means. And so we look up Exodus 4:6, which tells us that Moses' hand was 'leprous, as white as snow', and we consult Numbers 12:10, where Miriam is punished for disobedience, by being made 'leprous, as white as snow', and we begin to wonder whether 'white as snow' is actually a mark of judgment. Would this make sense of Isaiah 1:18? What if it is saying that those sins which are currently so prominent ('like scarlet') will indeed be judged? The word translated 'though' could equally be 'if', in fact it usually is, and hence the verse probably reads as a curse on the sin of Judah.

This makes perfect sense in Isaiah 1, which is a chapter relentlessly cataloguing the sins of the people in preparation for judgment. Whatever made us read it differently? Is it too far-fetched to say that once white people got hold of the Bible they simply assumed that an image of 'white as snow' would be a positive thing? Sadly, the evidence suggests that black and white imagery has indeed been interpreted by the (mainly white) scholarly tradition along these lines. A verse near the beginning of the Song of Songs has the female lover in the poem say, 'I am black and beautiful' (Song of Songs 1:5). But consult this verse in traditional English translations and it will say 'I am black but comely' (KJV), or 'dark am I, yet lovely' (NIV). The decision to translate the little linking word as 'and' or 'but' is really up to the translator. And who would find it a surprise that the woman is beautiful after saying she is black? We begin to see that it depends somewhat on the perspective of the interpreter.

These verses show us, not to put too fine a point on it, that interpretation is not always a matter of black and white. This too is something we will return to from various angles later on.

(7) *Psalm 46:10*

'Be still, and know that I am God!'
I remember a quiet meditative little chorus, sung several times over, and the entire lyric of which was these eight words from Psalm 46:10. What could be wrong with that? There certainly seems little problem with urging a little quiet acknowledgement of who God is in the midst of our busy and chaotic lives.

The world of Psalm 46, however, is unlikely to be one where we pause to sing this little ditty a few times over while we just move into a time of silence. It is a world of roaring waters, trembling mountains, nations in uproar, an earth in turmoil and desolation, and divine intervention in wars of all kinds. But, says the Psalm, none of these almighty phenomena are the bottom line: if you will only turn long enough from your CNN 24-hour coverage and screaming tabloid headlines, it is the Lord of Israel who will be exalted among the nations. But no one notices this because of the uproar. In which case, the way to read verse 10 is probably as an imperious shouted command to 'Be still!', or perhaps, in everyday language, to 'shut up!' Stop what the world is obsessed with, and take note of who is really in charge.

So is there then anything wrong with the quiet meditative little chorus? Is it saying something which is in itself true but which does not happen to be what the verse in question was about? And does that matter?

Our demo is at an end. Shall we be still for a moment of silence before plunging into the real thing?

STOP PRESS
DATELINE: A LONG TIME AGO
(IN A) PLACE: FAR FAR AWAY
SUBJECT: ABRAHAM'S DIARY DISCOVERED

The startling discovery of Abraham's personal diary provides a unique insight into the experience of God in ancient times. This from his old age:

'Get up and go,' he said.

'Leave your people, leave your land,' he said.

'Forget the dining table, three piece suite, photo albums, new patio, desirable residence in good school catchment area and neighbourhood watch scheme,' he said. 'And go.'

Easy for him to say.

I still get shivers up my spine whenever I hear him speak. This year it's a war against the local king cartel. That year it's trying to sort out little Lot's inept property deals and bad housing decisions. Those premiums on the Sodom Bank home insurance nearly ruined us, and then of course the whole episode with the angels. I have never been as exhausted as I was after praying for him that day. Family! You love them and you live with them, but they wear you out. Sarah still hasn't forgiven me for passing her off as my sister. And Isaac worries that I'll get so emotional over him that I'll do something seriously overzealous.

There are rewards of course. More blessings than I can count, although, as we say in our family, better a raisin cake in the larder than all the stars in the sky. Yes, these promises. I don't know what to make of them. Sarah says one day everyone will look back and say 'See how it all worked out!' I don't know. I suppose I believe it. But sometimes there's not much evidence.

A blessing to all the nations, indeed! 'Go among them and do not be afraid,' he says.

Easy for him to say. I'd like to see him try.

STOP PRESS
DATELINE: AD 95
PLACE: PATMOS
SUBJECT: HOLY BOOK UPDATE

With the release of 'Revelation' here on the Greek Island of Patmos yesterday it is rumoured that God has brought his so-called 'Holy Book' project to completion. This project, expected to be known as 'Bible' when published as a single book, has been in progress for hundreds of years now, having over-shot all deadline and budgetary predictions and having required all kinds of technological developments along the way to cope with multiple scrolls, authorship by committee, mass production, and the complex legal issues of divine copyright. In all these areas 'Bible' has broken new ground.

In a move which has confounded critics and supporters alike, the closing instalment ('Revelation') appears to be unlike most of the previous instalments, and religious groups have claimed that it contains material entirely unsuitable for family reading. A spokesperson said, 'The apostle Paul would never have written such sensationalist material.'

Equally controversial is the decision to release 'Bible' without a built-in back-up system of help pages. 'It's hopeless' said a spokesman for the church in Rome. 'If this book gets read by just anyone then who knows what it might be taken to mean.' It is widely thought that the deity will not be taking up his option on issuing an inspired guide to interpreting 'Bible', but commentators expect that a flood of human authors will be filling this gap in centuries to come.

In spite of the clamour for divine clarification on all these issues, God's only comment was reported to be, 'I have nothing further to add.'

Chapter 1

TRUTH, THE HOLY SPIRIT, AND OTHER MINOR ISSUES

'Bible Not Handbook for Living' Shock Claim

God did not write the Bible in English, which most English people believe was just an oversight. More confusingly, he didn't write it as a Handbook for Living. Just think how simple it would be to interpret the Bible if it looked more like this:

THE BIBLE
Section 1: God
Point 1: God is omniscient and eternal
Point 2: God created the human race

And so on right on down to:

Section 5973: Church Car Park Ethics
Point 649: But if the pastor has a second car then only one space should be held in reserve unless points 598 and 603 apply, or if it is the day of his MOT test.

Then, of course, we would not have people studying biblical interpretation, we would just have lawyers (and sometimes, in the New Testament, you will notice that these professions did get confused, which didn't help anyone, eg Luke 11:52).

More seriously we would have a Bible which would be wonderfully relevant for us but in turn irrelevant for everyone else who had ever lived. Church car parking wasn't an issue in the Middle Ages, and neither was recycling, nuclear war, which hymn book to use, which denomination to join, whether to shop on a Sunday, and so on. The idea of a Bible that tried to cover everything which might ever be relevant is simply a non-starter.

So instead we have a Bible which comes to us in a strange form from distant times and faraway places. It tells us ancient stories and includes letters, law codes, old songs, poems, dreams and visions. Which makes it a bit of a failure as a handbook, but much more interesting to read.

The Truth, the Whole Truth, and a lot of other things too

The way the Bible goes about revealing truth, instead of trying to be a handbook of truths, is that it shows us God. In the New Testament this becomes even more focused: it shows us Jesus. Jesus himself said, 'I am the truth' (John 14:6) which shows that he wasn't using the word 'truth' in the same way we do. We don't think of truth as something that applies to people, whereas in the Bible the idea of truth is linked with ideas like 'faithfulness' or 'keeping your word'. (Some people think that 'amen' is linked to the Old Testament word for truth, *'emet*, and means something like 'let it be true'.) When we think of truth this way it becomes clearer why Jesus described himself as 'truth'.

When we turn to the Bible we do indeed find that one of its major concerns is to reveal truth to us. But in fact God does a whole lot more in the Bible than just tell us truths. He also makes promises to us, he offers us blessings and even curses, he commands us, he comforts us, he invites us to worship or to praise or to repent or to grieve . . . And he does almost all of this through stories or letters or poetry or prophecies. So one of the basic things we have to learn when reading the Bible is what kind of writing we are dealing with in any particular Bible passage.

Context(s)

If in doubt always introduce a technical term. The technical term for 'kind of writing' is *genre*. Two modern examples of genre are 'science fiction' and 'murder mystery'. We are using our knowledge of different genres every time we ask, 'What kind of film shall I get from the video shop this evening?'

Knowing what genre to look for is a particular example of 'reading in context'. We all know the dangers of taking something out of context. With the Bible this is particularly easy to do since we are talking about a 2,000-year-old book and we are unfamiliar with its background. As we saw in the introduction, we have to look at the historical and cultural background of different Bible passages, as well as at the various effects which these passages have on us. Amongst other things, we will have to think carefully about what the *author* intended, what the *text* itself says, and what we, as *readers*, bring to the passage. Learning to interpret the Bible well is largely a matter of learning how to read it in its various contexts, and these issues will come up throughout this book.

STOP PRESS
DATELINE: 1270 BC
PLACE: PHARAOH'S PALACE
SUBJECT: ISRAELITE EXODUS – SOME PUBLIC SERVICE
DISRUPTION EXPECTED

Further to recent reports of bizarre meteorological conditions and freak events of nature in and around Pharaoh's palace, Egyptian authorities released a terse statement this morning to the effect that Egypt would not be trading on the international money markets today, owing to a sudden and unforeseen domestic labour shortage. Train and bus services are also expected to be disrupted and all flights in and out of Cairo have been suspended. Unconfirmed reports suggest that up to 600,000 men plus women and children – nothing less than the entire Israelite slave population – have departed Egypt in an almost unprecedented mass exodus during the night.

Shock waves from this event are already being felt in other centres of empire around the fertile crescent. A spokesperson for the Babylonians announced that security had been stepped up in Babylon, but declined to comment whether the Babylonian government would be attempting to take over the lucrative bricks without straw franchise which Egypt has to date monopolised in the Near East.

Other royal palaces have offered condolences to Pharaoh on the death of his son. A state funeral is planned for early next week.

Related news: Pharaoh's office has denied reports that its army suffered a major rout at the Sea of Reeds in the early hours of the morning, claiming that these reports are simply Israelite propaganda. 'This is just another pathetic attempt to distract attention from our good record on interest rates, expansion of the Nile Cruise business, and pyramid stock flotation,' said a spokesman for Pharaoh.

Why Bother?

Why bother with all this stuff about how to interpret the Bible? There is after all a lot to be said for just getting on with reading the Bible and not worrying about interpretation too much. But as we have already seen with some of our examples, it can be hard to read anything without some understanding of its context and background. In fact we are automatically processing background information every time we read the Bible, even if we don't do it very well. In this sense, interpretation itself is not the issue. We all interpret every time we read, but it's *better* interpretation that we're after.

Here are some less convincing answers to the question 'Why bother?':

1. You normally don't need to interpret the Bible, you just have to read it and do what it says – except when you get to a difficult or embarrassing bit, and then you need to interpret it, so that you can show why it doesn't really apply to you. So interpretation is for getting round the difficult bits and for explaining away all the things you wish God hadn't included. Like much of the Old Testament, for instance.

2. The reason why we need to learn how to interpret the Bible is so that everyone can see why I am right. Everyone else's view is just their interpretation.
3. Spending all our time arguing about how to interpret the Bible is a useful way to avoid having to do what it says.

And finally, the most unanswerable claim of all:

4. Hermeneutics is just a way of avoiding the plain, literal sense of the Bible. (Note that the word 'plain' is very important here: it implies that anyone who can't see it the same way is being deliberately difficult.)

None of these views takes seriously the fact that every time we read we are interpreting. Interpretation is not an optional luxury for those with nothing better to do. Interpretation is the window through which we see the Bible; it is the packaging that always surrounds the passage; it is the loyalty card that rewards regular reading; and it is the unseen guest at every Bible study meeting. Our aim is to make it a welcome guest.

Hermeneutics in the Bible itself

Another argument sometimes used against hermeneutics is that it is just a recent development which people used to do perfectly well without. Certainly, people have not always been willing to say that reading necessarily involves interpretation. But the practice of biblical interpretation goes right back to the Old Testament itself, to Nehemiah chapter 8.

Here the Jews have returned to Jerusalem after being in exile. They have been getting things like walls and taxes sorted out, and have now turned their attention to such matters as prayer and worship. It falls to Ezra to read to the assembled crowds from the books of the Law. (Ezra was a priest and teacher of the law who had come from Persia to help organise the Jewish people amidst the upheaval of their return to Jerusalem. Although he got a book of the Bible named after him, he actually missed out on most of what happens in it, and turns up a lot in the book of Nehemiah instead.) Anyway, Ezra reads and the Levites interpret the law for the crowds: 'They gave the sense, so that the people understood the reading' (v. 8). From this we learn, among other things, that they didn't find the Old Testament straightforward even when it was being written all around them.

So what do I need . . . ?

Here is where we list the tools for the task of biblical interpretation (not including the coffee, which goes without saying.) For some people this is a very short list: it only consists of the Bible, and everything else just complicates matters.

Well, yes, you certainly need a Bible. But perhaps the model of 'just me and the Bible' is too individualistic. I would like to suggest that one other important 'item' on your list is a friend, or preferably a church full of friends, so that you are not just trying to understand the Bible on your own, regardless of what God is also saying to those around you. Best of all will be a wise friend or two who are several steps ahead of you and can help you work things out, without always trying to get you to agree with them. With friends like this, you can discuss what you read, explore the various difficult questions which come up, and consider how God may be speaking to you through the Bible. And all the while they can watch out that you don't start developing some weird and wacky ideas such as European Monetary Union being a mark of the Beast, or thinking that standing up for truth means having violent disagreements with other Christians on points of doctrine rather than being a witness to Christ among those who do not know him.

Such wise friends are, in many ways, a short cut through the jungle of books and reference works which are available. Nevertheless, a good Bible dictionary, or some commentaries and study guides, can only help, and there are some recommendations for these at the end of the book. Reference books also do better than friends when it comes to remembering details over long periods of time.

The final thing on the list is God's help, through the Holy Spirit. In John's Gospel Jesus describes the Holy Spirit as our 'advocate', or 'comforter', or 'teacher'. In fact, in the context of John's Gospel, 'teacher' is possibly the best word for the Holy Spirit, since he will lead us into all truth (John 16:13), reminding us of all that Jesus taught, and teaching us everything (John 14:26). This puts Jesus at the heart of the Bible and the Spirit at the heart of interpreting it. Which is how it should be.

Unfortunately it also opens up the way for that most humble of all claims: 'My interpretation must be right because God told me!' There is no simple way of responding to this. 'But God just told me the opposite' is effective but may have the considerable disadvantage of not being true. 'If you look at the context then the passage can't possibly mean what you say it means' is often true but sadly it is not usually effective. So what to do? You could pray, or give them a copy of this book, or perhaps both. Perhaps one of the ways in which God 'gives' interpretations like this is through the accumulated wisdom of the church down through the ages. It is not that new interpretations cannot be right, but it does seem odd if 2,000 years and millions of people have all missed the point until now. So one practical response is to think about how well the proposed interpretation would have worked in other churches in other times and places. Sometimes, like the Psalm 46 example we considered earlier, what is being said is true, but is not based on the verse in question.

Chapter 2

LEARNING HOW TO READ: DIFFERENT TYPES OF CONTEXT

Have you ever watched a young child as they learn to approach different books in different ways? 'My First Book of Road Safety' just doesn't capture the imagination like 'Papa Elephant and the Missing Potty'. It requires a whole different set of reading assumptions and skills.

There is no way to break this gently, so here it is: being born again will mean having to learn to read again. At least if you want to get to grips with the Bible it will. 'My First Book of Tabernacle Dimensions' (Exodus 25– 31) also tends not to capture the imagination like 'The Prophets of Baal and the God Who Went to the Potty' (for yea, verily and forsooth 'Your God is on the potty' is a perfectly fair translation of part of 1 Kings 18:27).

Here we will look at how to read a passage from the Bible in context – or in particular in its historical, literary and biblical contexts. Reading a Bible passage in its proper context is sometimes called *exegesis*, which comes from the word meaning 'to lead out of', and hence means something like 'reading out of the text the meaning which is in it'. You can do this with any text, and it doesn't matter how much you agree with the text or think it is totally wrongheaded. An exegesis of the Communist Manifesto, for instance, will simply tell us what is in it, regardless of whether we happen to think that Marx was a genius or deluded. Likewise, biblical exegesis is, in the first place, a matter of finding out what is in the passage, not commenting on how encouraging or bizarre or important it is. With a little practice the words 'exegesis' and 'exegetical' can be dropped in at regular intervals to make it sound like you really know what you are talking about: 'I liked your sermon but I wasn't sure about its exegetical basis.' Try these for size: straightforward exegesis; exegetical foundation; exegetically far-fetched; caffeine-free exegesis . . .

Exegesis is a major step along the way to interpreting a passage, although it is not the only step. Once you have dug up the meaning of a passage you might still have a lot of other questions about how it applies to you, or how it fits with other passages. These are good questions, but they are not questions about exegesis.

That was then, but this is now

In Revelation 3:15,16 the risen Jesus says something to the church of Laodicea which I have never seen as part of any Christian worship song: 'I know your works; you are neither cold nor hot. I wish that you were either cold or hot. So, because you are lukewarm, and neither cold nor hot, I am about to spit you out of my mouth.'

This image of being 'lukewarm for Christ', while not very singable, is nevertheless a memorable one, and lends itself easily to a stirring sermon which asks us not to be lukewarm, but to be on fire for Christ. Not much wrong with that. But the verse is slightly odd when read from this perspective, since Jesus appears to be saying that he wishes the church in Laodicea was 'either cold or hot'. Wishing it were hot is something we can make sense of. It is less obvious in what sense Jesus would wish it were cold.

A last ditch attempt to salvage the 'on fire for Christ' kind of interpretation might say that it is better to know where you stand with Jesus: the one thing he really cannot put up with is people who do not make up their minds. So far so good, but 'better to be cold'? Could we really square this with the Gospels, or indeed with what we understand Christianity to be about?

Throughout the twentieth century, as the archaeologists moved in to the parts of modern-day Turkey where these letters from the book of Revelation were sent, a huge amount of information was uncovered about some of these places. In particular, they discovered that two of Laodicea's near neighbours were well known for their water supplies. Hierapolis to the North had hot water springs celebrated for their healing properties. Colosse to the East (which was the place where the letter to the Colossians was sent) had a cold water supply which was bottled as drinking water for the region. Laodicea had no water supply of its own, but instead it piped its water in from these two neighbours. And when it arrived it was, as you may by now have guessed, lukewarm. In particular, it was not 'hot' (ie good for healing) and it was not 'cold' (ie refreshing, good for drinking), and the only thing you felt like doing with it was spitting it out of your mouth. If only it were hot or cold; then it would be useful for something.

Set against this background, it seems more than likely that what Jesus is doing in Revelation 3 is taking a situation well known to the hearers of the letter, and comparing it to their spiritual life. The point is therefore not so much that they should be 'on fire' for Christ, but that they should be 'useful' for Christ, perhaps healing or refreshing to the life of the city. In this sense, of course, it is clear why Jesus would say that he wished they were cold rather than lukewarm.

This particular passage continues with many other examples of the same sort of thing. Laodicea was famous for the black woollen garments it produced, but Jesus invites them to buy 'white robes' from him. Laodicea had a famous medical school which produced an ointment for eyes, but Jesus requires them to obtain from him an eye-salve 'so that you may see'.

These are particularly clear examples of what is generally true: we need some historical information to help us make sure that we are dealing with the passage on its own terms. In other words: that was then, but this is now, and an awful lot has changed. This is the issue of *historical context*. It isn't the only type of context around, but it is one of the most basic.

How do I know what it's saying to me?

Reading the Bible in its historical context sometimes gets a bad press in the church, and it's easy to see why. It's harder than reading it out of context. It usually involves a bit of background work, which can lead some people to say that it is turning the Bible into a 'book for experts only', as if only experts could look up background information. And it will always trip up people whose idea of preparing a sermon is to read the passage through a couple of times in the car on the way to the service, no matter how passionately they may pray for wisdom. It is after all so much easier to say 'God is telling us to have a collection every week to raise money for the church, just as Paul said in 1 Corinthians 16:1' than to say 'Paul told the Corinthians to set aside money for a special collection for the struggling churches in Jerusalem, and from this we can understand some biblical priorities about giving . . .'

Of course, you can only get away with bypassing the historical context in certain kinds of passages. Consider verse 10 of the same chapter: 'If Timothy comes, see that he has nothing to fear among you . . .' You would soon find yourself in a tangle if you tried to preach a message along the lines of 'God is telling us to be prepared to look after Timothy': this verse is obviously not written for us. How then can you tell whether a passage is aimed at you?

A popular view is that if it would inconvenience you then the passage is not for you. People who adopt this answer have a great deal of tradition on their side. Unfortunately that doesn't count for much in this case.

Others say that it is the principles which count and the details are less important. There is something in this, but it still does not mean that we can avoid the questions of historical context or we might miss the principles altogether. As in the following example.

Who's wearing the trousers?

Consider the following quote from the Good Book: 'A woman must not wear men's clothing, nor a man wear women's clothing, for the

LORD your God detests anyone who does this' (Deuteronomy 22:5, NIV). There are all kinds of reasons why you might want to think twice about this verse, especially if you happen to be a woman who is wearing trousers when you read it. Of course trousers are not just 'men's clothing' these days, but they used to be, say 100 years ago. So you could try arguing that God, like pretty much everyone else, has just gone with the latest fashions. He used to find this kind of thing detestable but he doesn't really mind any more. Doesn't sound like there's much mileage in that, does there?

Alternatively you could try arguing that it was important then (whenever 'then' was) but that today it doesn't matter. Now this may be true but of course the verse doesn't actually talk about what is culturally acceptable, but about what God finds detestable. So this argument turns out just to be a long-range version of the first one.

If you're really ambitious, you could say that this verse was part of Old Testament law, but we don't live under the law any more – a good example of how to jump out of the frying pan and into the fire, which people do a lot with biblical interpretation. In this case, at least, there is no need to have a whole theory of how the Old Testament relates to us today before we can deal with just this one verse. In general this is just as well since the question of how much of the Old Testament relates to us today is a tricky one, and in practice very few Christians want to throw out all of it. That usually leaves them looking for reasons to throw out some bits and keep other bits, which leads to some highly selective hermeneutics. As this verse will show, we often do not need to go down that path at all.

The problem with all of these approaches is that they are not stopping to ask about the historical background to the verse before jumping in and assuming that we know exactly what it is talking about. In fact when Deuteronomy 22:5 talks about 'clothing' it is most likely referring to garments (or even just 'things') worn for magical rites. Probably this verse is forbidding performing magic as part of a fertility ritual for couples who wanted a child. And the God of the Old Testament was sure to find magic practices like that detestable, because they basically involved praying to another god.

Perhaps you should have been suspicious right at the start of this example. After all it involved just one sentence plucked out of thin air and giving you no idea of its context in Deuteronomy chapter 22. Consider the following sentence taken out of context from a recipe book: 'Beat until stiff and then stand in the fridge.' You can be sure that if this were a sentence from the Bible then someone somewhere would be trying to get a three-point sermon out of it.

STOP PRESS
DATELINE: AD 56
PLACE: CORINTH
SUBJECT: GOD CONDEMNS ALL RESTAURANTS

In a shock announcement today God has forbidden all people everywhere to eat in restaurants. He clearly states, in Paul's new letter to the Corinthians, that 'If anyone is hungry, he should eat at home' (1 Corinthians 11:34, NIV).

'This is a tremendous victory for us' said a spokesperson for the Christians Against Fast Food Coalition, 'although we had hoped that it would only apply to fast food chains.' Angry restaurant managers have claimed that this is just another example of Christian narrow-mindedness, and some have pointed out that there is nothing said in the passage to prohibit women from eating out. Some have even claimed that the relevant passage only prohibits hungry people from eating out, but that light snackers may be exempted.

The apostle Paul is no stranger to controversy. His statement to the Roman Christians that a man whose faith is weak eats only vegetables (Romans 14:2) led to a lengthy court-case brought against him by European cattle farmers. He was unavailable for comment last night since he was at a party thrown for him by the International Christian Hat-Makers Society, who are rumoured to have funded the publication of 1 Corinthians.

It all depends on how you tell it . . .

'Once upon a time there was a beautiful princess who lived with her ageing father in a castle on the top of a hill . . .'

These words clue you in automatically to the fact that you are about to read a fairy tale, and that asking questions like 'What was the constitutional status of the monarchy in this country?' or 'What did it mean in that culture to be beautiful?' will not help you much in understanding the story.

Sadly we don't have time to get into a fairy tale right now, so here is a biblical story instead: *'A man was going down from Jerusalem to Jericho, and fell into the hands of robbers . . .'*

This is the parable of the Good Samaritan from Luke 10, and once again we should find ourselves automatically aware that this is a story, and that we do not need to be asking how long the journey was or whether he was heading south or north. (Now in fact the road from Jerusalem to Jericho was a steep and difficult one and the journey was well known for being dangerous as it cut through remote mountain passes. But whether this helps you much in understanding the parable is debatable.)

Picking up these kinds of clues about what you are reading is being sensitive to the *literary context* of the passage. Often a few words is all it takes. Look at the opening of both Genesis and John: 'In the beginning . . .' Obviously here we are talking widescreen big picture stuff. The contrast between the beginning of John's Gospel and the other three Gospels is particularly clear. John is painting with big broad theological brush-strokes, whereas Luke, for instance, is telling us who did what and when (and how many different accounts he has researched too). The different openings invite us to approach each Gospel differently. By way of contrast, anyone starting at the beginning of 1 Chronicles will immediately detect that they are not browsing through the best-sellers section of the Bible.

Literary context is important. Becoming good at spotting different kinds of literary context is sometimes known as *literary competence*. This means not reading a parable as if it were history, or a poem as if it were scientific description. Literary competence is a skill rather than a process, and who we are makes a difference. Some people have pointed out the links between being sensitive to the passage we are reading and being sensitive to a person we are talking to. If we are good listeners, willing to let the other person explain their ideas in their own way without interrupting or assuming we know what they will say before they've said it, then we are also likely to be good readers, open to the particular concerns and ideas of a passage. These skills have a lot to do with being patient, gentle and caring enough to make sure we understand correctly what is being said. And since these characteristics are all something to do with the work of the Holy Spirit in our lives, there is a good case to be made that our spiritual sensitivity plays a part in how well we can read the Bible – which is a good example of how we need God's help in biblical interpretation.

STOP PRESS
DATELINE: AD 90
PLACE: JERUSALEM
SUBJECT: NEW GOSPEL TEXT FOUND

Great excitement here in Jerusalem yesterday at the announcement that a new gospel text has been discovered amongst the recently released collected papers of the apostle John. It is said to concern a story about a woman found committing adultery and Jesus' response to those who wanted to stone her. The story has been known in oral tradition for many years but has puzzled Christians by not turning up in any of the published gospels. With rumours growing that there will be no fifth gospel to go with the four we already have, and with Thomas allegedly way behind on his own gospel project, it had been thought that the story of the woman in adultery would not make it into the Bible.

However, sources close to John's literary estate announced yesterday that amongst his papers was this small fragment with 'This bit inspired' scribbled in the margin. There is some debate about where this new text fits with the existing gospel. Some have suggested that it should appear just before the 'light of the world' section. It is thought unlikely that it will remain as a separate fifth gospel when the completed New Testament is released, an event which is expected in the relatively near future.

Meanwhile the search goes on for the lost ending of Mark's gospel, thought to have been lost when the scribe who was copying it died from a snake bite.

It's all in the Good Book

'An eye for an eye and a tooth for a tooth', says the good book. Or did it say, 'Turn the other cheek'? Or was it both? They both seemed to make such good sense when we read them, but now we are wondering. Do these two pieces of ethical advice not contradict each other? Is our sceptical friend right with his claim that we end up just twisting the Bible to make it say whatever we want it to say?

Our sceptical friend has a point. Perhaps he has even found it convenient to put these two biblical sayings side by side in order to try and catch us off guard. A moment's reflection, however, or a frantic turn to a good reference book, perhaps, reminds us that it was in fact Jesus who first took this Old Testament verse about 'an eye for an eye' and contrasted it with his own teaching, in the Sermon on the Mount (Matthew 5:38,39). Does this just mean that he was contradicting the Old Testament? By no means! (This being Paul's regular response to just such a charge in his letter to the Romans). We will however have to understand two different contexts to be clear about this.

First we need the historical context of the verse taken from the Old Testament law. 'An eye for an eye . . .' was part of the Israelite attempt to bring in a fairer judicial system at a time when, for instance, stealing one sheep could lead to the wholesale destruction of the thief's family and property in revenge. The 'eye for an eye . . .' principle attempted to limit that kind of escalation of violence (eg Leviticus 24:19,20, one of the three places where the principle occurs).

Then we need to look at the *biblical context* of Jesus' teaching to see what he is doing. The Sermon on the Mount (Matthew 5–7) is where Jesus discusses the Jewish law and claims that he is fulfilling it himself (Matthew 5:17–20). In other words: in the same way that the prophets prophesied about him as the Messiah, so also the Law pointed to him as the one who would live the perfect life which God required. Just as the Israelite law had tried to set new standards for behaviour, so Jesus did the same. This much is clear even if we allow that there are many more complicated aspects to what is going on in the Sermon on the Mount. The important point here is simply that every biblical command occurs in some particular setting, and by selecting these particular Old Testament commands as he does, Jesus is deliberately making us ask questions about context and applicability, and not reduce everything to a straightforward 'the Bible says'.

Biblical context includes things like historical background and literary style, but it also takes seriously the way that the Bible functions as a single, unified and inspired book. Often the 'context' that matters most is how the passage relates to other biblical texts. The above example about the relationship between the Old Testament Law and the New Testament 'Gospel' is a difficult one, but it is a clear illustration of the need to see how each verse and passage fits into the bigger picture of the whole Bible.

The phrase *canonical context* is sometimes used to talk of this kind of context. The *canon* is the definitive list of books in the Bible as drawn up by the early church to settle the debates about what counted as inspired Scripture and what didn't. The fact that these have been noisy and sometimes explosive debates down through the centuries has nothing to do with the list of books being called a canon. We will come across an example of the importance of this kind of context when we consider Psalm 1 in a later chapter.

Chapter 3

THE BEGINNER'S GUIDE TO BIBLICAL GENRES

Having looked at historical, literary and biblical contexts, it is time to get down to some specifics and see what the different 'kinds of writings' (genres) that we find in the Bible actually look like. So welcome to this 'I-Spy book of biblical genres'. Score one point for each genre you find, and two if you can find one that's not in this list. We will start with things that look like stories, and then move on to things that don't.

History

History is such a broad category that it is almost useless as a genre identification. Nevertheless, for many people this is the big one, since *if it isn't history, it isn't true*. This is not a very good argument, because it confuses whether something *is* historical (experts like to call this *historicity*) with whether something *is trying to be* historical in the first place.

For example, suppose that someone wrote the book of Jonah as a story, to make a point – a bit like a parable in fact. Perhaps the point is to do with how you cannot run away from God, or that God wants people of all nations to hear about him, or that Jonah's self-centredness is a model of exactly what is wrong with Israel at the time. There are many possible points to the book of Jonah, and perhaps no one of them is the single 'right' one. The key is that hardly any of these points depend on whether the story told in the book actually happened or not, again just like the parables. Whether the shipwreck or the mass repentance of Nineveh actually happened turn out to have little to do with the truth(s) that the book of Jonah is trying to communicate. The idea that 'truth = historicity' is a classic case of getting into muddles with genres.

The Jonah example also demonstrates that 'Did it actually happen?' is not always the most helpful question to ask of a biblical story. In this case, we simply do not know whether someone wrote a story, or whether they tried to write down an account of events which happened to a real (historical) prophet. One might be wise to conclude, therefore, that there is not much point in wasting time on the 'historicity' question, but sadly, to judge from the amount that is written about it, this appears to be a much more pressing issue for some people than 'What is God like?' or 'What does it mean to offer ourselves in service to this God?' The historical and biological possibilities of a big fish swallowing a whole person end up becoming a major part of proving the credibility of Christianity: a tale every bit as bizarre as the book of Jonah ever was.

Narratives and Stories

A slightly more useful term than history is *narrative*, which refers to any section of literature written to tell (or narrate) a story. *Historical narrative* is a subset of narrative in general, where the story being told reports something which happened. Another kind of narrative is *mythical narrative*. 'Myth' means so many things to so many different people that it is perhaps worth avoiding the term, but defined positively, it refers to any great ancient story which tries to explain the way the world is or was. Defined negatively, it is 'a bunch of mystical hocus-pocus', like the world floating on a giant turtle, or angry gods hurling mountains at each other, and is used by some to suggest, simply, 'not true'. You should probably try to avoid confusing these two definitions. Mythical beasts and warring deities do not feature very heavily in the Old Testament, although towards the end of the book of Job we do encounter Leviathan and Behemoth, beasts of the land and sea thought to have been created on the fifth day (see Genesis 1:21), but on the whole not much is made of these ideas. This low profile would in fact have been quite a remarkable point at the time, and sets the Old Testament apart from many other ancient writings. This is also the place to note that fans of talking donkeys should check out Numbers 22.

Anyway, since much of the time we do not really know if the narrative is trying to report something that happened or not, these days the word *story* is used as an alternative to the whole debate about history. 'Story' in this sense has become, believe it or not, a technical word meaning 'a narrative which may or may not be historical but it doesn't matter anyway'. It doesn't matter because the powerful thing about a story is the way it captures your imagination and 'speaks to you', not what it tells you about the past. Is this development a good thing?

It is important always to answer a question like 'Is this a good thing?' by saying 'Well: yes and no. It all depends on what we mean exactly'. The word 'story' is not helpful if it means that we lose sight of the historical basis of the Christian faith, in the life and death and resurrection of Jesus. The stories told about Jesus in the Gospels are trying to show, at least in part, what really happened, especially concerning the resurrection. If it is *just* a story, and never happened, then this makes a very significant difference.

But on the other hand: yes, focusing on the story can be a positive thing. Sometimes we have little idea of the literary context, and we don't have a clue whether the story 'happened': there's simply no evidence either way. In such cases no one can say for sure whether it is the story or the history behind the story that matters. Books like Job and Esther fall into this category. Esther has a historical setting, but then so does *War and Peace*. The best way forward in such cases is not to worry about historicity too much, but to get on with enjoying the stories.

Gospels

Still on things that look like stories, there has been some debate about what sort of book a *Gospel* was in the first century world. Was it a biography? Was it historical or literary, or both? Is it a unique kind of writing that we only find in the Bible?

A few years ago the experts were generally going for this last option: we only have Gospels in the Bible and there is really nothing else like them. So everyone learned that Gospels were not biographies, because for instance they did not record the whole life of Jesus, or because they were organised around theological themes. Then the wind changed and it is now much more fashionable to believe that the Gospels are biographies again. Not like modern ones, of course, but nevertheless a lot like your average Greco-Roman biography. The chances of anyone catching you out by having a better knowledge of Greco-Roman biography than you do are, let's face it, pretty slim, so you can afford to sound fairly confident with this one.

Some people like to distinguish between the gospel of John and the other three, which are known as the *synoptic gospels*. This has nothing to do with the fact that it is impossible to provide a synopsis of Luke or Mark which is any shorter than the Gospel itself, but everything to do with the fact that 'synoptic' means 'seen together'. These three gospels cut and paste the same material in different orders. In other words, they all look at basically the same stories – they 'see them together' – and hence the name 'Synoptic Gospel'. John, on the other hand, tends to stick with altogether different stories. On the rare occasions when he does refer to an incident from the Synoptic Gospels, such as the feeding of the 5000, scholars have been known to call this an 'optical allusion'.

Parables

Parables, which occur mainly in the gospels, are little riddles or stories, told to make people think. Jesus used this teaching device a lot. Understanding a parable is a bit like getting a joke: you have to 'get the point' to see why it was told. This 'getting the point' is sometimes known technically as a gestalt moment, or less technically as an *a-ha!* moment, since when you get the point you usually say something like 'a-ha!' Whatever you call it, this is an important point in hermeneutics and we will come back to it later.

Not long ago it was fashionable to say that a parable could have only one point. This was a neat theory which did away with a lot of funny ideas about reading the parables as allegories. An *allegory* is where everything in the parable stands for something else, so that, for instance, the two coins in the parable of the Good Samaritan could represent two sacraments (!), or the two testaments, or the law and the gospel, or any other of the immediately obvious things that come to mind when you hear 'two coins'. So it seemed to tidy everything up to argue that a parable could have only one major point, until, of course, people realised that there was no evidence for this theory. For example, the parable of the two sons in Luke 15 makes at least two points depending on which son you identify with. The result: another well-established theory that everyone now tries to pretend that they never believed . . .

The 'We' Passages

One other type of narrative that is worth mentioning is the famous 'we' passages in Acts (Acts 16:10–17; 20:5–21:18, and 27:1–28:16). These unusual passages, written in the first person plural, are very short and were discovered by a Scotsman, hence their name. More to the point, the fact that they represent an eye-witness account written by someone who was there tends to provide yet more evidence, if it is needed, that the New Testament, and in particular the book of Acts, tells it like it was. The phrase that should trip off your tongue at this point is, 'Good indication of historical reliability.'

Letters

What is the Bible doing when it is not telling stories?

The main thing it does in the New Testament is give us *epistles*, which is the traditional name for letters. Epistles should not be confused with apostles, who were the people who wrote them. Usually we only get one side of the correspondence on these occasions, so reading a New Testament letter can be a bit like listening to one end of a telephone conversation. It seems unlikely that 'half a telephone conversation' will catch on as a genre description, but it does highlight one important point: these letters are written in response to some specific situation in the first century world. They are not 'timeless' statements of Christian doctrine, but particular arguments in certain contexts designed to have some very practical effects in the lives of the first readers.

Epistles come with a whole set of subdivisions which make up genres in themselves. These include:

- *Standardised introductions* – like To: church.god@corinth.com;
- *Further introductory thanksgiving* – except, most noticeably, in Galatians 1:6, which is a pretty big clue that when Paul wrote to the Galatians he was extremely annoyed with them;
- *Paraenesis* – the technical term for the bit of the letter which takes all the theological discussion and turns it into practical advice (and usually begins with a great big 'therefore' as in Romans 12:1);
- *Concluding exhortations* – the strangest of which is the last verse of 1 John. This is hardly a conclusion at all, but almost looks like another section of the letter which John simply never got around to writing (although probably what this tells us is that we are not yet very familiar with all the different styles of first century letters).

Apocalyptic

Despite its name, *apocalyptic* is not a style of pre-Caribbean rhythmic singalong, but a picturesque 'mark my words there'll be trouble ahead' kind of language. The Bible tends to use this at moments of extreme unease with the way the world is, such as in the book of Revelation, or the second half of Daniel after they ran out of Sunday School stories. 'Apocalyptic' literally means 'unveiling' (or 'revealing', hence 'Revelation'), and focuses on showing us the world in unfamiliar light through bizarre and spectacular imagery, in order to give us a fresh outlook on what is around us. Apocalyptic books often communicate through symbolism and imagery: this is usually a way of highlighting issues of good and evil, in unexpected places, rather than a code to crack where each symbol 'stands for' a particular person or country or group.

Apocalyptic should not be confused with the *apocrypha*, which is a collection of books mainly from the period between the Old and New Testaments. Apocryphal books tell Jewish and early Christian stories, report on prophecies, offer wisdom and advice (a bit like Proverbs), and can often be distinguished from the Bible by phenomena such as angels carrying prophets around or mysterious hidden scrolls revealing everything in numbers. As you can tell from this description, the same style of writing is still popular at station bookstalls today.

Old Testament genres

The Old Testament has a whole variety of genres besides the narrative parts. The most charming is the existential angst of Ecclesiastes. This, of course, is not a technical term for a genre, but rather alludes to the way that some people get so uptight about life that they dress in black with trendy haircuts and spend all their time sitting in cafés wondering why they exist. This makes it a fairly accurate description of Ecclesiastes, although we cannot actually prove that it was written in a café. The book begins with the startling claim: 'Meaningless, meaningless, utterly meaningless! Everything is meaningless.' Anyone trying to ignore the context of this verse and construct a three-point sermon based on it will soon be found out.

More generally we have *poetry*, particularly the book of Psalms, which turns upside down the concept of God speaking to his people through the Bible, since it is entirely composed of God's people speaking to God. The historical contexts of the Psalms range across several centuries, and are often lost in the mists of time. Although some of them come with handy titles like 'Written by David when he had a flat tyre in the wilderness of En Gedi', these are really guesses (sometimes good guesses, admittedly) which were added later, long after the Psalm had first come into circulation.

One of the longest poems in the Bible is the Song of Songs, which is mainly about how wonderful sex is. Many people have found it hard to believe that the Bible would ever say this, and so claim that it is actually about Christ and the Church. For this view to be convincing, you would really need quite a strong argument about how the *canonical* context of the book overrules all the other contexts, which is certainly debatable. More likely you could argue that the poem works both as a song of two lovers as well as an image of the relationship between God and his people (such as is used in, for instance, Jeremiah 2:2). Alternatively, of course, you could just enjoy what it says about sex.

The Proverbs are the clearest example of *wisdom literature*. They were usually short and memorable sayings composed by after-dinner speakers in the royal court of Solomon, many of whom appear to have had rather interesting experiences of marriage, hence the frequent references to wives as dripping taps or leaky roofs. The picture of the perfect wife in Proverbs 31, who is not only beautiful, widely respected, a devoted mother and a wise teacher, but also manages to make a profit before breakfast, perhaps also indicates some wishful male thinking. The perfect husband, by way of contrast, is conspicuous by his absence.

Prophecy plays a major role in the Old Testament canon. Most of what we call the prophetic books (eg Isaiah, Jeremiah) are collections of *prophetic oracles*, which were shorter sayings given on various occasions and edited together into the longer books we now have. This is why some of these books are difficult to read through in one go. The person who edited together a book like Isaiah is called a *redactor*. The person who reads an entire book like Isaiah straight through is called *tired*.

When the Jews put their canon together, the first books that they called prophecy were Samuel and Kings, which we call history. This is a particularly notable example of the fact that classifying books by genre is a tricky business.

Two other common genres are *legal codes* (like much of Leviticus and Deuteronomy) and *genealogies* (lists of family and clan names) which turn up in all kinds of places, including the very first chapter of the New Testament. These two genres were included by people who were worried that if reading the Bible was made too entertaining then people would stop believing that it was good for them.

STOP PRESS
DATELINE: 550 BC
PLACE: JERUSALEM
SUBJECT: 'EVERY DAY WITH LEVITICUS' – PRESS RELEASE

Stuck when your friends ask you about the regulations for mildew? Need help understanding the difference between clean and unclean animals?

The publishers of the highly popular *Build Your Own Model Tabernacle in 24 Days* are proud to introduce *Every day with Leviticus – a guide to daily living*.

Leviticus speaks powerfully into our daily needs. Be stimulated to a greater awareness of who God is, and what he requires of us. Thrill to the immediacy and challenge of the text. Its pages will grip you with terrifying intensity as you discover the astonishing perfection of God's holiness, explore the practical issues surrounding morality and ethics, and see the wonder of God's provision of atonement for us.

Also included:

- A cut-out-and-keep wall-chart on the regulations governing infectious skin diseases;
- Background to that controversial verse which states that when a man has lost his hair and is bald, then he is clean (Leviticus 13:40).

Every day with Leviticus is available at a festival near you.
Coming soon: *Through Hezekiah's Tunnel in Six Daily Readings*

For the advanced genre spotter . . .

Most of the genres listed above are fairly easy to recognise. But as a reminder that the Bible comes to us from an unfamiliar background, we will discover on looking more closely that there are various other recurring patterns in Scripture. Score extra points if you recognise any of the following.

Annunciation scenes typically feature an angel appearing in blinding glory with an urgent post-paid message from above. *Household codes* are lists of rules for family living, such as we find in Colossians 3:18–4:1. *Virtue and vice lists* (e.g. Ephesians 4:31,32) are a standard ancient way of contrasting different lifestyles, although you often only get the virtues or the vices separately, depending on the mood of the writer. In *prophetic commissioning scenes* a prophet discovers a job description sent from on high, and spies trouble ahead (eg Exodus 3 or Isaiah 6).

One of the most fascinating of all genres is the 'man meets woman at well' romantic episode. Isaac, Jacob and Moses all find wives this way (in Genesis 24, 29, and Exodus 2) so when Jesus meets the Samaritan woman at the well in John 4 the stage is set for a wedding . . . or is it? In terms of genre it is notable that Jesus does not marry the woman. In terms of the society of the time it would have been remarkable if he had. As a result of this tension, readers of the story are left wondering what Jesus will actually do. John 4 is a story of gender and racial boundaries being challenged time and again, as Jesus invites her into a different sort of relationship: an eternal relationship with God.

How to take care of your Genre Collection

After you have patiently spotted all these different genres, you may be wondering what to do with them. The important thing is to use them and not let them sit around getting rusty. What does it mean to 'use' a genre? The most important point of grasping the genre of a biblical text is that it helps us to let the text work on its own terms. The Christian habit of dividing up the text into lots of little pieces which we read one piece a day, such as we encountered in the introduction, has an unfortunate effect here. The basic danger it introduces is that of reading out of context.

Suppose you open up your Bible at Leviticus 3:16 and read 'All the fat is the LORD's'. This one verse might prompt you to lead a devotional talk at the next meeting of your local Christian Slimmers' Association, but alas you will certainly be missing the point. However, if you just read John 3:16 and talked about our need for God, or 2 Timothy 3:16 and talked about the authority of the Bible, you might get away with it. Why?

The reason is that passages in the Gospels or letters can communicate important messages in just a few words, whereas with genres like narrative (or legal codes, in our example) you need a longer passage to get the point. So taking care of your genre collection is a matter of practical importance. 'What God is saying to me' through any passage will be said in different ways depending on the genre of the passage. As a basic rule of thumb, to understand a parable, a prophecy or a proverb, read the whole thing. Since parables and proverbs are usually short, this is not normally a problem. However, to understand a story, you still need to read the whole thing, even though it may take a lot longer, as the following example demonstrates.

Gideon: the Founding Father of Fleeces?

Gideon's story is told in Judges 6–8, where he is described as 'a mighty warrior' by an angel who possibly had his tongue firmly in his cheek (Judges 6:12). The scenario is well known: unsure about whether God is really going to use him to deliver Israel, Gideon asks for a sign from God that will confirm his divine intentions. Can God make Gideon's woollen fleece wet and the ground dry overnight? Yes, he can. Still unsure, Gideon goes on to ask for the reverse sign. And God obliges.

Thus began a long tradition – which would surely astonish Gideon if he knew – of 'laying a fleece before the Lord' to test out what God wants. Since most modern Westerners do not have a handy supply of fleeces, they often take this metaphorically, and say things like 'God, if you want me to give money to the poor this Christmas, then please double my income first.'

How are we to evaluate this tradition in the light of the story of Gideon? In terms of the biblical story, there has been what experts like to call a 'hermeneutical leap' from the *story* of what Gideon did, to the idea that the Bible *teaches* us to 'lay fleeces'. Not everything that happens in a biblical narrative is a model for us. Later in the book of Judges a short-sighted judge promises to sacrifice to the Lord the first living thing he sees on returning home from battle, only to find that it is his daughter (Judges 11:29–40). Unsurprisingly, our hermeneutical muscles are flexed into shape very quickly by the prospect of applying this awful story to ourselves. Instead we conclude, rightly, that here is a classic example of what *not* to do. So the obvious question is: how can we tell whether Gideon's fleece is an example of what to do or what not to do? Perhaps it is neither. Perhaps it is just a record of what Gideon did.

How can narrative tell us anything? Probably not in short sound-bites but over longer passages where you get the big picture about what is and is not a good idea. The big picture which the book of Judges paints is this: Gideon, like most of the so-called 'heroes' in the book, is simply one more person God uses, in spite of their weaknesses, to do great things. So the narrative tells us lots of things, perhaps especially that God will use us despite our failings. But it does not teach us to lay fleeces.

Now if this is not the right interpretation, then when you wake up in the morning may this book be wet and all the books around it dry . . .

But how long is a long story?

Genesis is a tremendous story, with a great deal to tell us. However, to get it in focus we need to read all 50 chapters. If we focus on individual words or sentences too much, we will find all kinds of things God did not intend to say – rather like the preachers who enjoy telling you all about the significance of the badger skins in the tabernacle in the book of Exodus, but who neglect to mention the event of the exodus itself with all its extraordinary social and political implications.

But then, is reading the whole of a book like Genesis enough to settle any questions of interpretation which it raises? As a story,

Genesis does not really have a very satisfactory ending. This is because it runs right on into Exodus, and then goes on to make up the Pentateuch (the five books of Moses, up to and including Deuteronomy). In turn, the Pentateuch becomes part of what is sometimes known as the 'Primary History', so called because it is a history and, well, because it comes before everything else. This takes us as far as the end of 2 Kings. By this time you can see it coming: the best context of all for reading Genesis is to read it as a part of the whole Bible, seeing how it fits with everything else that God has chosen to say.

What we think God is saying through Genesis depends on the larger picture, or framework, within which we read Genesis. In principle he could be taken as saying a lot of different things depending on the context in which you are reading. He could be revealing the beginnings of Israel, or the story of why the world is in a mess and what he proposes to do about it, or the historical background to the Law, or how he works with such unpromising material as Abraham, Isaac, Jacob, Joseph and others, giving us hope that maybe he can even work through us. He is definitely *not* telling us where to go and search for the ark, or how to pretend to be your brother so that you can get your father's blessing, or how to lie about your wife being your sister, or how to laugh at angels. Keeping our genre distinctions clear can be a matter of great practical importance in biblical interpretation.

STOP PRESS
DATELINE: c1300 BC
PLACE: GOSHEN
SUBJECT: SETTLERS MOVE ON

In the wake of old Joseph's death recently, his extended family moved on last night after a tearful and emotional day of farewells, setting their sights on the long trek to Egypt and a new life of skimmed milk and low-fat honey. The family asked for no flowers, but made this heartfelt statement as they left:

'Now you've got to get this straight; it's pretty confusing. There's this promise see. God came down and spoke to Father Abraham and said, "You will have many sons", and I am one of them, and so are you, and, well, let's all praise the Lord. Anyway, Father Abraham was pretty old at the time, too old to have sons, but he did anyway, because our God is like that, but he had the wrong one first, called Ishmael, so he had to have another one, called Isaac. He was the right one, but he could never tell his twins apart, we all know how it is, and they didn't get on either, which didn't help, until finally one day the younger one, Jacob, stole this blessing from the older one, Esau, and so his Mum sent him away to be safe, and he met Rachel and had lots of sons, although the funny thing was there were lots of different partners involved, and it all got a bit messed up. Anyway, one of them, our father Joseph, was thrown into a pit, and he ended up a slave to Potiphar, and got thrown in prison, and started predicting the future in dreams about grapes and baskets, and ended up working for the Pharaoh, and doing this thing with fat cows, thin cows, and a centrally planned economy. We never understood that bit, frankly.

'And Abraham was promised this land, which is called the promised land, and his descendants will inherit it, but, well, all we have right now is Joseph's bones in a box. But the idea is to take this box up to the promised land, when it's ready. Except that the new Pharaoh doesn't know about this and has this really weird thing about making bricks without straw, which isn't going down too well, but apparently it's called capitalism and it's going to be really big.

'So, where are we? Well, we're not entirely sure what happens next. Can you blame us?'

Chapter 4

HOW TO GET HERE FROM THERE: AUTHORS, TEXTS AND READERS

There is a well known story about the man who was driving along one day and realised he was lost. Pulling over, he stopped a pedestrian and asked how to get to where he was going. The pedestrian thought about it and then said 'Well, you can't get there from here.'

The feeling that you can't get there from here is a familiar one for some Bible readers. How can my world relate to the world of the Bible? On the face of it, it is an uneven match. In the blue corner we have all the big questions: What is God like? What does it mean to be good? Should we always tell the truth? It is here that we put the Bible, the world's most read and most famous book, which has spoken to humankind down through centuries. It concerns itself with the great themes of God – creation, redemption, sin, suffering, good and evil, and the history of the world (at least a large chunk of the ancient world). This is home territory for the philosophers, the systematic theologians and the moralisers, offering a kind of cosmic OFSTED inspection. That's life in the blue corner.

Meanwhile, you are in the red corner. Right now, your world is concerned with things like finding a parking space, affording your weekly food, passing an upcoming exam, coping with a baby who won't sleep at nights, trying to find a job . . . You would dearly like God to speak to you on these issues, but whenever you read the Bible it appears to be preoccupied with these other, weightier matters.

By now, it seems to me, we should be suspicious of this contrast. What we have discovered so far about the Bible suggests that 'religious' is a label that fails to do justice to it at all. Does the Bible really belong in the blue corner? Where, in fact, does it fit most naturally?

Consider the story told in Joshua 2. Notice how Joshua sends two spies ahead of the people of Israel, with this very technical and confusing command: 'Go, view the land, especially Jericho.' Pause for a moment. If that were you, what would you do next? The Bible glides effortlessly along to its very next sentence: 'So they went, and entered the house of a prostitute whose name was Rahab, and spent the night there.'

Well, of course, in the long run it works out. Rahab gets praised for lying (James 2:25) and observant Christians ponder on the unlikelihood of God using a prostitute. What is not often noticed is that God uses two men whose idea of spying out the land is to visit her in the first place. By the time the Israelites settle in the promised land, the roll call of the people God has chosen to use includes prostitutes, astrologers, pagans and (to stretch a point) donkeys. Encouraged? Or do you still want the blue corner?

If the Bible is in fact more like this, then perhaps we can begin to get some idea of how to 'bridge the gap'. In looking at the questions of reading in context and understanding different genres, we have really only been thinking about the 'back then' part of hermeneutics. The question of how to bridge the gap between what was going on back then in the world of the Bible and what is happening now in our own lives is one of the major concerns of hermeneutics, and it is the one which will occupy us in this chapter.

What does it all mean?

We will make a start on this task of bridging the gap between then and now by looking at how we discover the meaning of a Bible passage in practice. There are three places to look for the meaning of a Bible passage, not counting those study Bibles that come with extra notes printed at the bottom of the page which give you the 'answers'. You might find the meaning there of course, but that's not what we are talking about at the moment.

The meaning of a passage, basically, depends on:

- What the author wanted to say
- What the words and sentences in the passage mean
- What the readers understand as they read.

Indeed, it usually requires a bit of negotiation between the three things: author, text and reader. We will take them one at a time, and see how they all contribute to the meaning. After looking at them in turn, we will then consider how we may have answered the question of how to bridge the gap.

Getting inside the Mind of the Author

One of the important questions about the meaning of a text is what the author meant, or intended, when he wrote it. This 'authorial intention' is a key ingredient in understanding the Bible.

For some people the meaning of, say, Romans 1:16,17 is whatever Paul had in mind when he wrote that 'I am not ashamed of the gospel; it is the power of God for salvation to everyone who has faith . . .' This is definitely a good start, although it needs tightening up a bit, since Paul could have been thinking of all sorts of things as he wrote. Perhaps he was wondering whether he would finish the letter in time to make the last post, what he was going to say in next Saturday's sermon, or maybe even when he was going to stop feeling queasy from the eggs he had for breakfast. Paul may have had all these things in mind but they do not have much to do with the meaning of Romans 1:16–17. However, by and large, it is always a worthwhile question to ask what the author had in mind when he wrote, or, more precisely, what the author intended to communicate.

One advantage of this approach is that it cuts out a lot of weird and wacky interpretations that rely on ideas like the author of Revelation knowing all about the Gulf War, or Moses having an opinion on the National Lottery. One disadvantage is that it appears to leave you and the Bible back in your opposing corners, not really on speaking terms when it comes to the modern-day issues you are facing. So what other ways in might there be?

Meanwhile back at the text

The belief that the meaning of a passage is linked to what the author was trying to express is sometimes known as *romanticism*. At the opposite end of the spectrum, for the less romantically inclined, we find *structuralism*. Now this is an extremely impressive word to learn since virtually nobody knows what it means. In fact the only people who ever did understand it wrote books on it, and there were only a couple of them, making it one of the least widely believed 'ism's of all time. For our purposes we can simplify hugely and say that structuralists believe that it is not the author's intention that matters, but what the text actually says.

You may think that there is not a lot of difference between these two things, but there turns out to be a fair amount of difference. A lot of things an author wants to say he does not come out and say explicitly. You have to read them between the lines. A lot of the things we want to say about the Trinity, for example, are between the lines in the Bible, which makes hardly any clear statements about the Trinity. As another example, a structuralist would be suspicious of the view we mentioned earlier that the Song of Songs is all about Christ and the church. A romanticist, however, might be happier with it, which just goes to show that romanticism and romance are not the same things at all.

Even combining the author and the text, we still find that the bridge between now and 'back then', between us and the Bible, is a shaky one. You may find that the Bible has a lot to say about relationships, for example, but what you want is for it to say something about *your* relationships. How can it do that? There is one obvious part of the picture still missing, and it is the part where you come in: the role of the reader in interpretation.

STOP PRESS
DATELINE: AD 75
PLACE: ROME
SUBJECT: NEW SECTION OF LUKE'S GOSPEL RELEASED

Work continues on Luke's Gospel here in Rome. Dr Luke released his trial text yesterday for what is projected to be the beginning of chapter 15. Text follows.

Now all the double-glazing telesales people and drug addicts were hanging around Jesus wherever he spoke. And the Christians, especially the ones who studied the Bible a lot, were getting fed up with this and saying, 'This fellow welcomes druggies and even goes down the pub with them.' So he told them this story.

'Which one of you, having a hundred clients and losing one of them, doesn't leave the ninety-nine on hold and go after the one that is lost until you get a new deal? And when you have signed the contract, you take it home rejoicing. You call together your friends and neighbours, saying to them, 'Have a drink with me, for I have renegotiated the deal we lost.' In the same way, there will be more joy in heaven over one drug addict who sorts himself out and makes a few changes to his life than over ninety-nine Christians who don't need to change.

'Or what teenage girl, having a complete set of earrings of her favourite boy band, if she loses one of them, doesn't turn off the stereo, turn up the lights, and pull her bedroom apart until she finds it? When she has found it she calls her best friend on her mobile and tells her the whole traumatic story, and they go out and buy another poster to celebrate.

'In the same way, the angels are turning up the celestial stereo every time someone sees the light.'

The reader responds . . .

The bridge between here and there, between now and then, becomes crossable when we realise that we are part of the process of interpreting the Bible. The Bible is communication with us, and we play a part in making that communication happen every time we read it.

This is part of the reason why we never reach the point in the Christian life of saying, 'Well I've read the Bible now, so what next?' There is always more, because every time we read the biblical text it communicates with us in a new way.

Most people who read the Bible have one very good question in mind: 'What does this mean to me?' Taking this question as far as it will go, some people have argued that the meaning of a text simply is whatever the reader gets out of it. This view not only moves away from authorial intention, but it also goes beyond what the text says explicitly, and finally asks, 'What effect does this passage have on me?' This fits nicely, of course, with postmodernism as a general philosophy, which is basically the view that the only standards which matter are the ones which help you get on with life, so if it works for you then do it. Anything goes and truth is whatever you make it. When it comes to interpretation, the bottom line, which is a fairly flexible one, is the reader's response to the passage.

Before we rush to evaluate this we might note that it corresponds quite closely to the average small group Bible study which so often begins with those fateful words, 'Is anyone struck by anything in this passage?' Such a question focuses immediately on the reader's response. At times this can be helpful, especially if the point of the passage is to provoke you or make you change your attitude, as with the parables, for instance.

Consider the parable of the two sons in Luke 15. Let's imagine two people: one is broke, drunk and a long way from home – we will call him Mr Smelly. The other is older, a respected Christian who enjoys his Sunday service as well as his Sunday lunch – Mr Comfortable. Now if Mr Smelly could somehow hear Jesus' wonderful words across the centuries then he may well run to the arms of his Father in heaven and gratefully accept the offer of forgiveness for his sins. Then he is stuck with the task of finding a church which will be equally as forgiving. And when he rolls up on Sunday morning, then the parable goes to work on Mr Comfortable. What it most probably does is point an accusing finger at him for his unwillingness to embrace Mr Smelly, either literally or metaphorically, before he hurries home to the Comfortable house for his roast dinner.

Now what is the *meaning* of this parable? The meaning for Mr Comfortable is the accusing finger pointing in his direction. It is not an abstract meaning which he might enjoy discussing over lunch, especially if Mrs Comfortable, who remembers the parable only too well, invites Mr Smelly round for lunch that day. The meaning of the parable for her might have been that she should break the habit of a lifetime and invite someone she did not know to her house that afternoon. The parable has no meaning which can be separated off from the response it provokes. You can bet that the Comfortable family will not be having an abstract discussion about parable interpretation that evening. They are more likely to be feeling the heat from the way that the parable has invaded their lives and changed them forever.

What of Mr Smelly? Well, what goes around comes around, and one day he may be comfortable too. Then who will he be lunching with? Once you have walked into its world, this parable will never let you go.

This example demonstrates that what the reader brings to the passage affects what he or she will take away from it. Clearly this is a long way from saying that a reader can take away anything they like from it. The reader may be limited by the text, but not limited to just one right meaning. An emphasis on the role of the reader, therefore, does not imply that anything goes. Recall the delightful old rhyme that says, 'Wonderful things in the Bible I see, most of them put there by you and by me.' Some readings are just plain wrong, whether they are to do with seeking out the spirits of the dead, supporting apartheid, or taking fellow Christians to court. On most matters, however, interpretation is not as clear cut as this.

Does the Bible encourage wise financial investment or carefree giving with no worrying about tomorrow? The answer to this depends a bit on what kind of framework you bring to the Bible, or the kind of lifestyle or attitudes you have concerning money. Very likely there is more than one valid viewpoint. You may be the kind of person who needs to learn how to give, give, give, or perhaps instead you need to learn how to stop getting into debt. What the various Bible passages on this topic mean to you depends on who you are as a reader.

Crossing the Bridge

Hearing God's communication is a bit like any conversation where you both come with an agenda. You have things you want to talk about and God has things he wants to talk about. At times the difficulty of genuine communication can be very frustrating. However, developing the competence to be a good Bible reader involves learning both how to talk and how to listen. There are times when it is important to bring your frustrations and problems to your Bible reading and match them up against the attitudes talked about in the passage, like with the parable of the two sons. You should expect the passage to 'speak to you'. At other times it is good to learn how to listen to what is on God's agenda, which may be something you had never considered before.

The meaning of a Bible passage is not just pinned down to what it meant then or what it means to you now: it is an active thing which depends on you and God communicating together as you read. Sometimes you will discover that although you can after all get to here from there, God may have in mind some altogether new place where he wants you to be.

There are two things that kill off Bible reading. The first is not bothering to read it at all – a very quick way of losing interest in the Bible. The second, which is more subtle, is to read it assuming that you already know what it is all about and not expecting to hear anything new. In between these two extremes is the chance to build the bridge between the world of the Bible and your own world, and to cross it, to whatever strange new place God has in store.

STOP PRESS
DATELINE: TUESDAY 12TH SEPTEMBER 823 BC
PLACE: MOUNT CARMEL
SUBJECT: FIRST RAIN FOR 3 YEARS AFTER BAAL PROPHETS
ARE MASSACRED

COPY FOR TOMORROW'S EDITION of ISRAEL TELEGRAPH
From our Royal Correspondent

Astonishing scenes on Mount Carmel yesterday heralded the return of the Yahweh prophet Elijah after several years in the wilderness, and an extraordinary confrontation between him and the prophets of Baal. King Ahab, who watched the whole affair from the Royal Box, was on his way in the so-called Ahab-mobile to Jezreel, further inland, when thunderous storms broke over the whole country, ending the three-year drought which had so seriously threatened the land.

Elijah's challenge to the prophets of Baal to present themselves and call down rain from heaven was taken up in force, and there were an estimated 400 of them yesterday on Mount Carmel. But their sacrifices were to no apparent avail, until Elijah intervened.

Fire from the Sky

When Elijah stepped forward, there was a sudden release of fire from the sky which burned up the sacrifice he had placed on the altar at Mount Carmel.

Speculations about Elijah's motives are focusing on his long-running dispute with royalty, and his well-known claim that Yahweh, the God of Israel, is siding with the ordinary Israelite and will not accept the royal abuse of privilege. Elijah's opposition to the ruling élite has had him in trouble before, notably with Queen Jezebel.

An official statement from the Company of Prophets should be released today, but a spokesman said that they did not wish the public to think that their organisation was necessarily committed to the line Elijah was taking: 'It's all very well for him turning up after three years eating locusts somewhere in the desert, but I think he's out of touch with the complex political realities of contemporary prophecy.'

Rain details and weather forecast to follow

News agencies report the following headlines for tomorrow's other editions:

Elijah Wins Showdown of the Prophets as Rains Return to Israel – *The Independent Israeli*

Minister of Agriculture quits but claims, 'My faith in Baal was a personal matter' – *The Israel Times*

Shekel crisis in wake of shock rains threatens Israel's membership of single Near Eastern currency – *The Israeli Financial Times*

You're Fired! says Eli – *The Israel Sun*

Is Your God on the Loo? asks Prophet – *The Israel Sport*

Chapter 5

THE SCIENCE AND THE ART OF HERMENEUTICS

The Parable of the Sausage-Making Machine and the Art Gallery

Hermeneutics: art or science?

For some people, producing interpretations of the Bible is a bit like making sausages. You take a large amount of meat, put it into your sausage-making machine, and pull the right switches. Out come sausages, in a user-friendly form. Likewise, you take a large amount of biblical text, put it into your hermeneutical machine, and pull the right switches. Out come interpretations in a user-friendly form (often with three points all beginning with 'P'). Who you are does not make any difference: all you need is the ability to pull the switches.

Other people object to this. The competence to pull the switches is not just a skill anyone can develop, but it also involves who you are. In some ways, this goes back to our point about being sensitive to the passage, being a good listener, and being open to hearing unexpected and perhaps challenging points. So it makes a difference, according to this view, whether or not you are open to a spiritual relationship with God, because if you are not then no amount of switch pulling is going to enable you to hear God's voice emerge from your Bible study. People who argue this way see hermeneutics as more of an art than a science, and interpreting a Bible passage as a bit like appreciating a painting.

Both these viewpoints have something going for them: this is another case of 'both/and' rather than 'either/or'. The problems arise when people only see hermeneutics as mastering a set of methods for producing interpretations, or alternatively when they see a relationship with God as something that you bring as the over-riding framework to your Bible study rather than seeing it as some-thing which also grows out of (and is shaped by) Bible reading.

The Three Easy Steps to Biblical Interpretation . . . ?

Focusing on methods, then, can be good or bad. In practice it fits in well with an instant culture such as ours which likes to have things set out in easy steps. Thus we have plenty of books with titles like *The Seven Simple Steps to Making Your Church Grow* or *Five Formulas for Powerful Prayer*; and now, of course, *The Three Easy Steps to Biblical Interpretation.* (It is difficult, in contrast, to imagine a best-selling title like *A Hundred Hints for Hermeneutical Happiness.*)

One well-known model for biblical interpretation breaks the process down into three steps: observation, interpretation and application.

(1) Observe what is in the text;
(2) Interpret the details you have observed;
(3) After interpreting, apply the text to your own situation.

This, to use the image of the sausage-making machine, is the scientific approach that involves pulling certain switches in the right order and watching the 'meaning of the passage for today' drop out at the end of the process. We should say that these three steps can be very helpful in certain ways. However, they cannot be separated out into simple stages that we go through in order to interpret a passage correctly. Why not?

The main problem concerns how to work out what we should be looking for. Consider the example of 1 Corinthians 14:26, where Paul says to the Corinthian church, 'What should be done then, my friends? When you come together, each one has a hymn, a lesson, a revelation, a tongue, or an interpretation. Let all things be done for building up.' Some people read this verse and immediately see it as a description of how a church should organise its worship services. Regardless of whether what is described is a good framework for organising a service, we should remark first that such an interpretation has made one key move which is often not noted. It has assumed, or decided, that Paul really meant to use the word 'should' in this verse. (Of course the grammatical details are different in the Greek text, but this does not affect our point here.) This reading effectively works on the understanding that the verse says 'When you come together you *should* have a hymn, a lesson . . .' I have used this example in many contexts, and some people do not accept this point even when the vocabulary is discussed: they reply that obviously Paul meant 'should' otherwise why would he say it? Why indeed? It is not too far-fetched to argue that Paul is actually not that pleased with the church in Corinth, whose services are chaotic and do not bring glory to God, with one person shouting away, another breaking into prophecy, others singing hymns at the same time, and no one able to follow what was going on. Instead, Paul urges, each one should do what they do in an orderly way: one at a time, so that everyone can listen to, and thus be blessed by, each other. On this reading, verse 26 above is simply the preparatory description of the chaos before Paul goes on to say what should really be happening. Perhaps people take the verse as a prescription because they have already decided that if something is said in the Bible then it must be some kind of a model for us. The important point to note, then, is that the disagreement over how to handle this verse cannot really be decided by asking about observation first, and then going on to discuss the interpretation of what we have agreed upon. We cannot in fact agree on it without already bringing in a large amount of interpretation, and in this case the disagreement stemmed in part from differing understandings of the nature of how to 'apply' this verse to today.

There are other potential difficulties with seeing interpretation as a matter of these three steps of observation–interpretation–application. We may, for instance, not be aware of the points which the passage is responding to, but which are not spelled out. This is sometimes known as 'mirror reading' a passage, looking for the kind of agenda it might have had in its original situation in order to explain why it makes the particular points it does. An example of some of the things Genesis 1 might be responding to is given below.

Knowing what to look for in a biblical passage fits with the more artistic side of hermeneutics. In practice, we get most of our ideas about what to look for from other people, or from the books we read. Indeed this is probably as it should be. It is not an individualistic model. Rather, biblical interpretation occurs in the company of the whole church, under the guidance of the Holy Spirit, and in the context of learning from each other.

The real benefit of something like the three-step method is more modest. It allows us to check on what we have done after we have done it. It tells us when our 'observations' were really interpretations. It tells us, for instance, whether Paul used the word 'should' or whether we added it in. But even then there is nothing in this method that will settle the question of how significant our observations might be. As with any method, we cannot avoid having to use our own judgement at some point.

STOP PRESS
DATELINE: UNKNOWN
PLACE: DIFFICULT TO PIN DOWN
SUBJECT: 'I CREATED WORLD', SAYS GOD

In a new, highly poetic introduction to his ongoing 'Holy Book' project, released today under the provisional title 'Genesis 1', God reveals one of his most startling claims yet: that he created the world. 'I was fed up with people worshipping all the stuff I made, like the sun and the moon and the sea and the land, as if they were gods, so I decided to set the record straight,' he said.

This latest revelation is bound to be controversial. Critics have been quick to point out that God's decision to use the imagery of 'six days of creation' lays himself open to a somewhat literalistic interpretation. Others have claimed that the phrase 'male and female he created them' is a simple surrender to feminist pressure in the wake of the controversy over the 'woman came from rib' theme in the famous Garden of Eden story.

But many were clearly very happy with the account. Yesterday an unidentified priestly source said, 'We all found the worship of creation very distressing. After all, no intelligent person goes around worshipping trees. We're very relieved to see a clear statement here that the sun should not be considered a god any longer.' However it is doubtful whether the human willingness to worship created things will be dealt with quite so simply. Tree-worshipping communities were preparing counter-suits this morning.

A-ha!

Careful observation and interpretation will help us tune in to the wavelength of a passage. As we read and reread the biblical text, we begin to bring it into focus. Eventually, we become quite good at seeing it in its proper contexts and understanding what is and what is not significant about it. Each time you read the text, it changes who you are, and shows you more clearly what to look for. So when you come back and read it again, it looks different and you are changed again. This is one reason why there is something new in the Bible every time you read it.

This process of you reading the text, and the text changing you, and you reading the text again, is referred to as the *hermeneutical circle*. This has been thought to sound a bit too much like a vicious circle, and since every time you go round the circle you learn more and improve your understanding of the passage, many prefer to call it a *hermeneutical spiral*.

At some point, as you go up this spiral, you experience an a-ha! moment. This moment – impossible to describe but equally impossible to forget once you have experienced it — is when the passage suddenly 'makes sense', or 'falls into place', or 'speaks to me' (depending on what kind of church you come from). It is much more difficult to have an a-ha! experience if you don't know what you are looking for, but it does happen.

STOP PRESS
DATELINE: AD 1515
PLACE: WITTENBERG
SUBJECT: NEW INTERPRETATION OF ROMANS OFFERED

Martin Luther, the 31-year old lecturer in Biblical Studies at the University of Wittenberg, has argued this week for a whole new approach to our understanding of Paul's letter to the Romans. Contrary to the standard idea that the righteousness of God revealed in the gospel is what condemns us because of our imperfection, Luther is arguing that the idea of God's righteousness is a positive one.

Although he has yet to publish his ideas, students this week were reporting that Luther saw God's righteousness as *justifying* us in spite of our sin. 'Justification by faith', he is said to have claimed, makes sense of Paul's letter to the Romans only if it means that God freely justifies sinners who do not deserve to be made righteous.

That this is not the standard position of the church hardly needs emphasising. A spokesman for the church suggested that talk of a reformation of official church teaching was premature. 'I'm sure it will all blow over,' he said.

The Science and the Art

We have seen that the sausages we make with our hermeneutical science need supplementing with a more artistic outlook. When observing a painting, we do not go through a checklist of questions such as (1) What colours are most prominent? (2) What types of brush strokes are most in evidence? (3) Are any of the images given prominence? Instead, we stand back and get a feel for the whole work of art. Only then, in the light of the big picture, can we do the stuff about brush-strokes and colour tones.

In the same way, we need to get a feel for the overall thrust of a Bible passage – its basic ideas and teaching – before looking carefully at the details. There is no short cut to 'getting a feel for the Bible' except by reading and studying it regularly, and thinking creatively about what it says and how it says it. And keeping an eye out for those 'a-ha!' moments.

The View from Here

One question you may have at this point is: 'It's all very well to say, "Think creatively", but how can you do that in practice? Do you simply sit around and wait for inspiration to strike?'

Of course, it is very helpful when inspiration does strike. But one hint for learning how to look at Bible passages in fresh ways, or to get inside the way the characters work, is to try and see the story from someone else's point of view. Most biblical stories come with a point of view. The exodus, for example, is a great moment for the Israelites, but not for the Egyptians. Sympathy for the Egyptians may not be the point, but it might help us get under the skin of the story if we try to reimagine it from their perspective. We did that with this very example in an earlier part of the book.

The technical description for reading a passage this way is reading it 'against the grain'. Fortunately, you do not need to know that.

STOP PRESS
DATELINE: AROUND THE TIME OF ABRAHAM
PLACE: THE VALLEY OF SIDDIM
SUBJECT: POLICE ID ON SUSPECTS FOR SODOM AND
GOMORRAH BOMBING

Further to the devastation of the cities of Sodom and Gomorrah reported earlier, police have issued profiles of two men they wish to question. They were last seen drinking cappuccinos late Monday after-noon at the roadside diner out near Zoar.

The diner's owner reported that the taller of the two had seemed especially irritable. He had looked distracted and preoccupied, and had complained bitterly about the phone system being down again. He had wanted to contact someone called Lot, but was unable to get through. The shorter one, he added, was slightly overweight, and had spent his whole time poring over passports which, it is now known, were the fakes used to gain entry into the city. Both men had talked about a third member of the party, who had apparently stayed behind at Mamre and had been last seen talking to Abraham.

Lot is presumed dead in the aftermath of the bombing. Police are still wanting to contact Abraham. Motives for the attack remain unclear, but police said today that the explosive used in the blasts was extraordinarily powerful, and had left virtually no traces of where it might be from. The search for survivors goes on, but as a police spokesperson said, 'It would be a miracle if anybody survived this.'

Chapter 6

INTERPRETING THE BIBLE (1): READING A PASSAGE

We conclude with examples of two different ways of taking the Bible on its own terms. In this chapter we find ourselves a spot in the shade of the tree that dominates Psalm 1, and look at how we might bring together some of the things we have looked at by actually interpreting a biblical passage. In the last chapter, we will consider how to handle the Bible when our concern is to think about a particular issue. In each case, we are thinking primarily about questions of interpretation. Psalm 1 invites our attention because it is about living happily and hermeneutically ever after.

The Tree by the River

[1] Happy are those
   who do not follow the advice of the wicked,
or take the path that sinners tread,
   or sit in the seat of scoffers;

Psalm 1 opens with a description of a happy person. The theme of the Psalm is 'How to be Happy'. (Actually, in some translations, the word is 'blessed' which has the advantage of sounding much more religious, but the standard disadvantage of not meaning as much to most people.) The happy person is the one who does not let their life get dominated by the wicked, the one whose agenda is not set by the 'sinners' they mix with. Their agenda is set somewhere else.

²but their delight is in the law of the LORD,
   and on his law they meditate day and night.

Here we discover that their agenda is set by meditating on the 'law' day and night. The Hebrew word for 'law' here is *torah*. *Torah* meant 'instruction' as much as it meant 'law', and in Israel it was the name for the first five books of the Scriptures from Genesis to Deuteronomy (variously known as the five books of Moses or, in Christian tradition, as the Pentateuch). These include the 'law' of Moses on which Israel based its daily living, and it seems likely that this specific law, or set of laws, is in view here. So verse 2 is saying: the Torah is what it is all about if you want to get happy.

Now this could easily come across as a bit depressing. In fact you can already hear the preacher gearing himself up for the awful conclusion: just read your Bible every morning and every night and you too can live happily ever after! But we should be suspicious of this claim, because (a) it is not quite what the verse says, since it does not in fact mention either 'reading' or the 'Bible', and (b) it is a Psalm, and not a legal code, and is therefore more likely trying to paint us a picture than lay down a law. The picture comes in verse 3:

³They are like trees
   planted by streams of water,
which yield their fruit in its season,
   and their leaves do not wither.
In all that they do, they prosper.

The image is of someone who is like a tree beside a river. Their roots are down in the watered soil. The fruit appears in due season. This, apparently, is what it is like to meditate on the Torah.

If we go straight for our scientific hermeneutical approach, we may be led astray here, concluding that the application of this image is that we should read the Bible every day and thus be happy. This is fair enough as far as it goes, especially if we accept that the last verse of the Psalm gives us a rough idea of what it means by happiness:

⁶ for the LORD watches over the way of the righteous,
    but the way of the wicked will perish.

But the power of this tree-by-the-river image will (surprise, surprise) only come by meditating, or at least reflecting on it – rather as the Psalm itself suggests. If you think about this Psalm, let its image become part of your thinking, and really get inside it, then: a-ha! – the text will seize you. Once it has done that it will never let you go. On the other hand, if it never does grab you, then you can read Psalm 1 as often as you like and it will never be much more than a nice little poem at the beginning of the Psalms.

Hermeneutics with Roots

Perhaps, then, rather than asking 'what can I observe in this text?', we should reflect on 'what kind of a-ha! moment am I looking for?' What is the clue to the big picture which this Psalm paints?

The clue is not in how often you read the Torah, or how well you avoid the advice of sinners. The clue is in the roots of the tree. If you start from the roots and work outwards and upwards, then the rest of the Psalm will fall into place. A-ha! It's all about hermeneutics with roots.

If the tree is healthy and its roots are well-nourished, it will produce fruit and it will produce it in season. There are no short cuts and no tricks the tree can use to produce extra fruit on demand. Compare this with someone whose approach to the Bible is: 'I need God's help right now to make this decision about my job/buying a car/who to marry . . ., so I'll spend a day praying and reading the Bible and ask for God's help.' What kind of tree would this be? One which dumps a whole load of water on its roots in the hope of producing fruit in double-quick time. But of course, producing fruit does not work that way. You cannot shower the tree's roots the day before the harvest and expect it to make a difference. In the same way, someone whose biblical roots are firmly established and well-nourished can be confident about making decisions, because to them God's promise is that the fruit will come in season: the right outcome will come at the right time.

Spirituality, says this Psalm, is a matter of looking after your roots. This may or may not mean a Bible reading every morning and evening, but it does mean doing whatever it takes to keep your biblical roots in good shape. What this suggests in practice will depend to some extent on you, the reader, but it is obviously important, because it is basically about your spiritual health.

Hark! I hear the Canon . . .

What about the context of the passage? We do not know much about its historical context. Its literary context helped us to recognise that this poem is not a law for us to obey. However, the most important context in this case is the canonical context, or where it is placed in the finished Bible.

Psalm 1 is deliberately placed at the beginning of the book of Psalms as a kind of introduction concerning how to use the rest of the book. Christians down through the centuries have often found the Psalms to be great resources for meditation. This, we now see, is not because they give you applications to work on, but because they provide nourishing soil for your roots, which changes who you are (and thus propels you on to the hermeneutical spiral in a positive upwards direction).

The significance of the canonical (biblical) context goes even further. When the Jewish people organised their Bible, they did not do it in the same order in which Christians organise their Old Testament, even though it contains basically the same books. Jewish tradition put it in three parts:

- The Torah (Genesis-Deuteronomy, the '5 books of Moses');
- The Prophets (which included most of what we call the histories);
- The Writings (everything that did not qualify for the other two sections).

The Torah was the foundation of the whole Jewish scriptures. The Prophets began with the book of Joshua, and the Writings began with the book of Psalms.

Now in Joshua chapter 1, Joshua is commissioned by God after Moses' death. And what does God say to Joshua? In verse 8, he says 'This book of the law (= *torah*) shall not depart out of your mouth; you shall meditate on it day and night.' Where have we heard that before? We have heard it, more or less, right back in Psalm 1. So what we find is that both the other sections of the Jewish Scriptures start with a reminder to meditate daily on the Torah. It is difficult to imagine a more Scripture-centred approach to the idea of living a life to please God.

Hermeneutics in an instant society

Psalm 1, therefore, pulls together a lot of the things we have thought about. It suggests a way we can be changed as people. It gives us a picture of learning to think biblically. And, as we are changed, so our meditation on the Bible will continue to nourish us, helping us to go around and up the hermeneutical spiral – in other words, we keep on getting more and more out of our Bible reading.

Our ability to understand the Bible as God's book is all a part of our spiritual growth and our relationship with God. This is so different from the attitude of our slot-machine instant culture which likes everything, including the spiritual life, to be programmable and to offer instant results. It would like a nice methodology which allows you to put the Bible passage in at one end and produce a handy interpretation complete with practical applications at the other end.

This does not seem to be what 'being biblical' is all about when you come back to the Bible itself. Instead the Bible invites us into a lifelong process of change and growth. We put our spiritual roots down in biblical soil, and entrust ourselves to God to see where our faithful interpretation will take us.

Chapter 7

INTERPRETING THE BIBLE (2): UNDERSTANDING AN ISSUE

Sometimes our agenda is set by a particular Bible passage, such as when we are preaching or leading a study on a particular biblical text. Other times we bring our agenda to the text. We have already looked at the strengths and weaknesses of these two different approaches. Here our goal is to show a little bit of what is involved in studying the Bible thematically: how do we understand an issue in the light of the Bible?

Obviously there are many types of issue which all require different approaches. We could consider an example which is prominent in our world today but not particularly prominent in the Bible. How could we build on just a few verses to cover a large and complex topic today? To some extent this is the situation with current Christian debates about homosexuality, which is not a major focus of biblical texts. Cases such as cloning present more complicated scenarios still, where the Bible does not even come close to a discussion of the matter. A second type of example might be a case where an issue looms large in the Bible but is not a major feature of contemporary discussion. The biblical agenda puts practices like forgiveness and non-violence very high up indeed, but few churches give the impression of valuing them more highly than views on sexuality or worship styles. The issue we will consider, all too briefly, is what the Bible has to say on men and women, or male and female. This touches on today's concerns with gender, sexuality and ideas like feminism, while still offering a lot of material in the biblical text to consider.

Interestingly, this topic also highlights another shortcoming of the 'observation' model we discussed earlier. What if one of the really significant things about large parts of the Bible is the absence of women? Is that a feature of the text?

To keep our study manageable we will look at just a few key passages and try and show what lines of thinking emerge.

Male and Female He Created Them

Genesis 1:27 puts male and female together right at the moment of creation. In terms of canonical context, this is about as prioritised as it is possible to be. We will be aware that Genesis 2 then seems to zoom in on some of the details of creation and tell the story again, from a different point of view. In Genesis 2 the man is made first, and the woman taken from his side, or rib. So are men and women equal in creation or not? There are two arguments which people tend to use either way: who was created first, and who did the naming.

If Adam is made first does this in some sense make him 'better'? Is Eve the afterthought, or is her late arrival simply evidence that the man could not survive on his own? The Bible is unclear on the significance of this. In Genesis 1 the build-up of the chapter clearly indicates that what comes later is more significant than what comes earlier. Should we carry the same argument over to Genesis 2? Probably not. In chapter 2 the order is man – animals – woman, and it seems clear that the animals are not understood as more significant than either man or woman.

Some people argue that Adam has some kind of authority over Eve because he names her, just as he names the animals. There are several judgments that go into this argument, and we need to divide them up carefully in order to evaluate what is going on. Let us assume for a moment that naming indicates authority, even if anyone who ever named their baby and watched them grow up into a teenager may find this a pretty large assumption to make. 'Adam' is in fact ambiguous in Genesis. It means 'man' in Hebrew, and Hebrew operated with the same convention that English used to have, that 'man' could mean 'human' indiscriminately, so that women got to be honorary men too. As a result, it is not always clear when the passage is saying 'Adam' (as a proper name) and *adam* (i.e. 'the man'). Some people argue that until Eve is 'extracted' from Adam, the 'man' is simply a human: that it does not make sense to talk of male or female when there has only ever been the one of them. More straightforwardly, the name 'Eve' does not occur until Genesis 3:20, which is where we read that 'the *adam* named his wife *Eve*' (because 'Eve' sounds like 'living', and she is now to be the mother of the living). If naming indicates authority, then clearly that is what is occurring here, but of course something rather significant has happened between this point and the creation of the woman in 2:23. Back at 2:23 the delighted, and presumably exhausted, post-natal *adam* declared, 'She shall be called woman (*isha*) for out of man (*ish*) she was taken'. No Eve, no naming, just a kind of matching pair: *ish* and *isha*, man and woman, and a 'she shall be called'. The naming is at 3:20. What has happened in between is the minor matter of eating the fruit of the tree of knowledge. If naming is the issue then it does not happen before the 'fall'.

Here then are the created man and woman, back at the beginning of the earth, made in the image of God. Equal, but different, and thus in some ways, of course, not quite equal.

Creation and Procreation

In Genesis 1:26 humankind is given dominion over all the other living creatures. In other words: humans are in charge. (It seems likely that this is at least part of what it means to be made 'in the image of God', as in Genesis 9:6 which lets humans exact God's punishment precisely because humans are now in charge.) In verse 28, just two verses later, the commission to work has become more specific: 'Be fruitful and multiply'. In between came the verse about 'male and female'. A careful reading of these verses in context suggests that it is being male and female which is the key to the focus of the new command: one of the things men and women are supposed to do is have children.

The woman of Genesis 2 is then created as Adam's 'helper'. There is a big debate about what it means exactly to 'help'. I could help you achieve something you are doing, where I am in a secondary role. I might proof-read your letter or essay. It is still yours and all I am doing is offering a bit of help. On the other hand, I might help my child with their maths homework. In fact, I could do the sums in half the time, but my goal as 'helper' is to guide the child's understanding toward something which I already know. As in English, so in Hebrew. To help may or may not imply that the helper is in some sense 'subordinate' or inferior. (Note too that in the Old Testament God is often described as a 'help' to Israel, e.g. in Psalm 33:20.) Some people argue that the helping which Eve provides for Adam is the one thing which a solitary human could never do: it is the help of reproduction. There is some evidence for this in the way that the curses of Genesis 3 relate to the man and the woman: the man will have to work hard all the days of his life (3:17) while the woman will have greatly increased pain in child-bearing (3:16). Could it be that these specific curses are precisely related to the female role in creation of bearing children?

In 1 Timothy 2:15 we find the startling verse that 'she [woman] will be saved through childbearing'. At least one possible interpretation of this somewhat obscure verse is that it simply takes the Genesis narrative at face value and thinks that the calling of woman is to bear children – not every single woman, obviously, for even in biblical times they had spotted that that did not happen, but as a general description of what women do that men do not do. We may not find this a very appealing philosophy, nor a very comforting interpretation of 1 Timothy 2, but our point is to try and follow the lines of thought of the biblical authors first, regardless of how appealing we may find them.

What do men and women do in the Old Testament?

This may seem a slightly odd heading. The short answer is: they do just about everything. The list of what men do would go on almost as long as the Old Testament itself, but of course that is partly the point. The Old Testament is in many ways a book about God and *men* in a way that it is not equally about God and women. Having said this, women do end up doing a great deal.

Women are leaders. Miriam is a leader in the book of Numbers, and is listed as such in Micah 6:4. They are 'judges', in the sense of the book of Judges where the word means something like 'saviours' (of Israel). Deborah is the well-known example, from Judges 4, where we also come across a woman called Jael who marks herself out in a memorable tent-peg-through-the-head sort of way. In 2 Kings 22:10–20 we have the story of Huldah, a prophetess. At the beginning of 1 Samuel we meet Hannah, whose prayer is key to setting in motion the chain of events which unfold in the books of Samuel. Women also serve as heroines, in a couple of cases succeeding in getting books of the Bible named after them: Ruth and Esther. There was something else . . . What was it? Oh yes, women also have lots of children.

The hermeneutical question is: What do we do with all this information? We might note that it complicates a somewhat common argument about men and women in the Bible. Sometimes people say that the Bible may be very male-orientated and not give much space to women, but that is because it was a product of its time and women simply did not do then half the things which we now know they do. This list of examples suggests a possible counter-argument: the biblical authors were all perfectly well aware of women as leaders or prophets or heroines, but they told few stories like this precisely because they did not think that this was the generally appropriate role for women. These stories, if you like, would have been exceptions in cases where men had failed to do what was expected of them. Yes, there are women in prominent roles in the Old Testament, but the point might be that there are very few of them.

As always, the reader has to judge which of these interpretations is more likely. What seems obvious to us is not always a particularly useful guide in making judgments like this. In the midst of all this Old Testament male and female activity, we might discover several women who are noted as 'beautiful' (*yapheh*), such as Rachel (Gen 29:17), Abigail (1 Sam 25:3), Esther (Esther 2:7) or Bathsheba (2 Samuel 11:2). It is one thing to note that artists down the ages have portrayed these women as beautiful by painting them in the style of their own day. Is beauty in the eye of the beholder? It is slightly more disconcerting, at least to many male readers who have been enjoying these paintings, to note that the same word appears in the text to describe several men: Joseph (Genesis 39:6) and David (1 Samuel 16:12) being just two examples. Beautiful men? Do our translations say 'handsome' just because the translators do not think 'beautiful men' is quite right? Does it matter what we think is 'obvious' about this: did the Hebrews evaluate male beauty in the same terms as female beauty?

Questions of authority

Perhaps one way of getting beyond our listing of things women did or did not do in the Bible is to ask about those passages which declare what they should or should not do. In other words, what if we turn from the narrative sections of scripture and look at the pre-scriptive (or directive) sections. The classic passage for this discussion is one we have touched on several times before: 1 Timothy 2:8–15.

Verse 11 of this passage gives us a very clear example of wondering what we are supposed to notice: 'Let a woman learn in quietness with full submission'. We may jump to the word 'submission', perhaps reacting quite negatively to it, although 'submission' may not have been intended to indicate 'enforced submission' but something more like 'respectfully'. Perhaps. Several people argue, however, that what is really striking in this verse is the opening 'let a woman learn'. In a world where many women were not educated, simply by social convention, here is the biblical author taking a counter-cultural position and urging that they should indeed learn. What sounded like a concession is perhaps a stunning and liberating command.

However, it is verse 12 which is the real focus of attention. Here

Paul says 'I permit no woman to teach or to have authority over a man; she is to keep silent.' So much has been written on this one verse that we could almost have spent this entire book illustrating all our points from just these few words. I shall content myself instead with just a few outrageous over-simplifications.

- Is this Paul's personal preference ('I do not . . .') or a command for all? Probably all. The fact that a biblical writer says something in the first person is not usually understood as undercutting its inspired status.
- Is 'woman' here to be taken in its more restricted sense of 'wife' – could the verse be referring only to women teaching their husbands? Grammatically possible, but unlikely given the context of the passage concerning public worship.
- What does 'teach' mean? I want to say: 'it means teach,' but there is, to be fair, a debate about whether it refers only to 'accredited' authoritative teaching.
- What about 'authority'? The word means various things in the first century, ranging from any kind of teaching, right through 'authoritarian' (i.e. heavy-handed) teaching, even in one exceptional case to 'murder', which is about as heavy-handed as you can get.
- The word for 'silent' – could it mean 'appropriate quietness' rather than silence? Yes, it could.

Where does all this leave us? In a book on hermeneutics, I think it leaves us aware that there are plenty of reasons why people take different views on the kinds of issues raised by this verse. If this were a book on interpreting 1 Timothy 2, or on men and women before God, I would attempt to defend one particular interpretation, but my conviction is that sincere readers of this passage may in good conscience make different judgments about what is the best interpretation. The options involve either saying that this passage sets down a divinely inspired command that women should not teach men, backed up by the (somewhat obscure) argument from Genesis which follows in the next three verses; or that the verse, properly interpreted, only forbids certain types of (authoritarian) teaching; or that the verse was specific to a particular context (in Ephesus, where the letter of 1 Timothy was sent) and does not apply today. There are of course lots of variations on these positions.

It is a further matter as to whether anyone can really be so sure of their interpretation that they should judge other Christians according to whether they agree with it. Here grace may be the better part of hermeneutical wisdom.

Some Hermeneutical Reflections

Four concluding hermeneutical reflections as we consider how we have used the Bible in trying to understand this issue.

Firstly, note that we took Genesis seriously in our interpretation, but this did not involve us having a view one way or another on whether the stories of Genesis 1–3 are historical or not. Jewish tradition does not take them as historical, while Christian tradition has, in the past at least, been divided. You may have noticed that the rest of the Old Testament never once alludes to the Adam and Eve story, which should make us pause before saying that we cannot understand the Bible without a particular view of the creation stories. They seemed to do OK in the rest of the Old Testament at least.

Secondly, we have touched on the difficult question of how to balance out narrative texts with prescriptive texts. Paul's teaching seems to say one thing, while in the book of Acts he is shown operating alongside women (such as Priscilla) who seem to be acting with authority, and teaching groups of men and women, and Paul seems to go along with that. Perhaps Paul had not read his own letters? Whichever way you end up evaluating it, one lesson is clear: it is essential to take on board as wide a range as possible of relevant biblical texts in understanding an issue. There were many more which we could have looked at in this chapter.

A third question, a little more reflective on ourselves as readers, is to ask who set the agenda for the particular questions we asked? We looked at issues of authority, or naming, and of roles of women in the Old Testament, partly because these are the standard issues people raise in discussing our topic, but also because the reason that they become the standard issues is that they are notable features of the text. Nevertheless, perhaps there is space to ask about whether the men who have dominated the history of interpretation have inevitably skewed the kinds of question we ask. The preoccupation with authority, for example, may reflect male priorities more than female ones.

Finally, a brief note on feminist hermeneutics. 'Feminism' means many different things to different people. There are liberal feminists, Marxist feminists, evangelical feminists, and pagan feminists, to name but a few. The overall label 'feminist' may not therefore be particularly helpful, but whatever variety of it is in view, the underlying issue being raised is something to do with the importance of women's perspectives and experience in our thinking.

Feminist hermeneutics interprets the Bible with the working assumption that at least some of the things the Bible says about women were just part of the presuppositions of the ancient culture the Bible came from, and are not what God was revealing. This includes such striking biblical observations as women being the weaker sex and wives being told to obey their husbands, as well as the issue of not having authority over men.

Opponents of this approach say that it makes the Bible totally subjective because you can then disregard whatever bits you dislike. Defenders may point out that a comparable approach has been taken already with issues like slavery. By now we are aware of the fact that the issue is not whether the approach is subjective, because any interpretation which involves human beings is subjective, but whether the particular judgments involved are good ones. This is a much more tricky issue, and therefore does not get discussed as often. In some ways the special case of feminist hermeneutics highlights many of the issues we have been concerned with in this book, and the discussion about how to weigh up interpretations is precisely the discussion we have been learning to have.

What we have tried to model in this chapter is how to take as broad a biblical perspective as possible and trace a particular theme through the whole Bible. There are a lot of themes and a lot of Bible to keep us all busy for a long time to come. We have really only scratched the surface of it in this book. We have tried to grasp how the Bible can work with its remarkable mixture of simplicity and complexity. This is the big story of God and the creation of the world, and what happened next. It is a story of how Jesus came to reveal God in new and unexpected ways. It is a story which invites us to think of how we can live out our lives with this same God. Sometimes words and sentences from this story strike us with an unnerving power and authority. At other times we are puzzled, or intrigued, or simply left wanting to know so much more in order to interpret what lies before us. Whether looking at the big picture or the details, this book has attempted to introduce you to the wonderful, sobering, perplexing, challenging and delightfully strange new world that we find within the biblical text. May you dwell in it all your days, until the tree of Psalm 1 turns into the tree of life of Revelation 22:2, and our wisdom shall be complete.

Appendix

BIBLE TRANSLATIONS: A BRIEF SURVEY

The Bible was originally written in:

Hebrew	Most of the Old Testament, except for:
Aramaic	Ezra 4:8 – 6:8, 7:12–26; Daniel 2:4 – 7:28 and one or two verses elsewhere (eg Jer 10:11)
Greek	The New Testament (which also contains a few words of Aramaic, eg Mark 5:41)

Aramaic was a Northwest Semitic international language of trade and communication. It is perhaps best to think of Hebrew as a local dialect of it (which would make sense of, for example, 2 Kings 18:26). The Greek of the New Testament was the normal ('common') language of the first century AD. Whatever we may think about the inspiration of the Bible, it did not extend to having a special or perfect language in which the Bible was written, nor in fact did it extend to avoiding grammatical mistakes, but that's another story.

Most of us, of course, will be reading our Bibles in a translation, which is a long and honourable tradition stretching right back to the New Testament, where they mainly read the Old Testament in translation (the Greek version of the Old Testament being known as the Septuagint of the third or second century BC, usually abbreviated to LXX, which turns up frequently in footnotes in your average Bible translation). So one obvious question is: which translation should you read?

The best advice is to make sure you read at least two different ones, to avoid selling your soul to one particular translation. In this book I have mainly quoted from the NRSV (New Revised Standard Version, 1989). This is good for a balance between technical accuracy and readability, probably stronger on the former, and hence good for study. It was known upon publication as an 'inclusive language' translation, eg it opts for 'brothers and sisters' where the original is a generic 'brothers', and it will often pluralize to avoid male-specific language ('Happy are those who do not follow the advice . . .' in Psalm 1:1, for example, instead of 'Happy is the man who . . .'). Fifteen years on this is much more standard than it was, and a lot less controversial, though the NIV (New International Version, 1978) got into a lot of trouble in some parts of the world when it tried to introduce an inclusive-language version (now known as the NIVI). This year a fully revised edition known as the TNIV (Today's New International Version) has been published in the UK. A more recent attempt to go back to word-for-word correspondence is the ESV (English Standard Version, 2001). This may be fair enough for some study purposes, but it does go against the understanding of most who have worked in translation or linguistics, where word-for-word correspondence is normally understood to be less significant than idea-for-idea correspondence.

But it's tricky. If you live in a culture where a wise person will build their house on stilts to avoid the floodwater, do you translate Matthew 7:24 as 'a wise man who built his house on stilts'? Does that get the point across? Do you then miss the connection when Jesus says to Peter 'on this rock I will build my church' (Matt 16:18)? It doesn't really work to say 'on these stilts I will build my church' since the point in Matthew 16 is partly to do with a word-play between Peter (*Petros*) and rock (*petra*). Word-for-word translation can also create new problems even while it tries to be faithful to the words of the original text.

Both the NIV and the ESV opt for more conservative theological views in translation in general, with the NIV self-consciously attempting an 'evangelical' translation. This means they tend to be theologically clear, but do not alert the reader to why anyone would ever understand a verse differently. The NRSV or RSV (Revised Standard Version, 1952) is still perhaps the happiest mix of technical accuracy and readability. Other possibilities include:

- The REB (Revised English Bible), an attempt to pull back from the unusual NEB, ending up not unlike the NRSV overall.
- The NEB (New English Bible) which was full of oddities though fresh in places
- The Jerusalem Bible (and its update, the NJB), an excellent Catholic translation which is the only mainstream one to retain Hebrew names for God, thus 'Elohim', 'Yahweh', etc, making it especially useful for OT study.
- The CEV (Contemporary English Version) which reads very well and avoids sounding too 'churchy', but does this at the cost of leaving some verses quite rewritten from their originals.
- The GNB (Good News Bible), which is straightforward but not ideal for study, because it often significantly interprets (and sometimes over-simplifies) the text for you rather than simply telling you what it says.
- The KJV (King James Version, 1611), much-loved by some, much the cause of frustration and incomprehension to others. It was also known as the AV ('Authorised Version'), but this means that it was authorised by King James and not by God. Despite its glorious poetry it can lead you astray either because we now have a better understanding of the Hebrew and Greek, or better ancient manuscripts, or because the English language itself has changed, as for instance when the KJV talks about the friends of the paralysed man not being able to get near Jesus because of the press (Mark 2:4).
- The Message, a paraphrase written by Eugene Peterson, which is a wonderful and startling rendition of the text, guaranteed to make you think 'does it really say that?' and send you back to other translations to check, which can only be a good thing

Specifically for Old Testament study you should note the following:

- JPS ('Tanakh') edition – by the Jewish Publication Society (there is also a NJPS)
- The Schocken Bible – vol. 1 *the Five Books of Moses*, by Everett Fox, an attempt to produce a Jewish-flavoured translation, which really brings out the ancient feel of these Jewish Scriptures.

GLOSSARY

For those who have no time to read entire books, just memorise one definition a day to stay ahead. Some of these we covered in the book, some we didn't, but they are all something to do with the science, and the art, of interpretation.

Allegory

The idea that a story about one thing is really a coded way of talking about another thing. For example, Jesus tells a story of different seeds and soils in Matthew 13 but he is really talking about how people respond to God. Reading the Bible as allegory is very handy whenever it seems to be talking about rape, murder, holy war or some other noble human activity, which it does embarrassingly often for those who prefer to think of the Bible as 'religious'.

Authorial Intention

The authorial intention of a passage is whatever the author intended to say, except in the case of Jude 3 where the author tells us that he has not said what he intended to say but has written about something else instead.

Biblical Interpretation

The process of understanding the Bible, which may be a science or perhaps an art. This is not exactly the same as hermeneutics, which is really a broader word referring to the whole question of how we can decide what makes an interpretation a good one or a bad one. But in general you can get away with confusing them as long as you speak confidently enough. Which of course is what has happened in this book.

Clarity of Scripture

Surprisingly, this is not the idea that everything the Bible says is clear. It is rather the view that enough biblical teaching is clear and straightforward for us to live our lives faithfully in the light of God's Word. It was developed during the Reformation in response to the view that only experts could interpret the Bible. Given this, it is hard to explain how some reformers managed to find all sorts of passages which, they claimed, were 'clearly' about the awfulness of the Pope.

Eisegesis

A made-up word designed to contrast with *exegesis*. To accuse someone of *eisegesis* is to charge them with the crime of reading in to a text something which is not there. Eisegesis is very common in *proof texting*. In fact, it is just very common.

Exegesis

Derived from the Greek meaning 'to lead out of', hence the process of drawing out (or reading out) the meaning of the text.

Four-fold Meaning of Scripture

In the Middle Ages, it was common to argue that there were four levels of meaning in any passage:

- The **literal** meaning – what the text meant in its historical context;
- The **allegorical** meaning – what it referred to in the grand scheme of Christian doctrine if interpreted symbolically;

- The **moral** meaning – interpreting any passage for the individual in terms of what it could say about daily living;
- And the obscure **anagogical** (or **mystagogical**) meaning – covering whatever the other three left out, and relating it all to the future.

Thus 'Jerusalem', under this scheme, meant the literal city of Jerusalem; the church (allegorically); the individual soul (morally); and the heavenly city to come. It was a bit harder to say what, for instance, Zechariah's two olive trees stood for (Zechariah 4:3–5), but then not even the angel who showed them to him knew that, so perhaps it is an unfair example.

Fundamentalist

Anyone more conservative in their interpretations than you are is a fundamentalist. (see also *liberal*)

Hermeneut

This delightful, although increasingly unfashionable word, simply means 'one who does hermeneutics'. It can therefore mean 'interpreter' or 'exegete' or any of the other things we do when we are working on the Bible. 'Although I am an inexperienced hermeneut . . .' will dazzle your audience long enough for you to get away with whatever outrageous point it was you wanted to make.

Hermeneutical Circle

See hermeneutical spiral.

Hermeneutical Spiral

See hermeneutical circle.

Hermeneutics

What this book is about. Concerned with weighing up (biblical) interpretation, although sometimes used just to mean 'interpretation.' Also . . . on second thoughts, just read the book.

Illumination

After *inspiring* the Bible, the Holy Spirit has not decided to move on to more general miracle-working and prophetic ministries and leave the Bible to take care of itself. Instead, he continues to shed light on what he has inspired. This is what is known as *illumination*.

Inspiration

Belief in the inspiration of the Bible does not refer to the fact that it is full of really inspired ideas, but rather to the notion that the biblical text is 'God-breathed', ie exactly as God wanted it. The word translated as 'inspired' in 2 Timothy 3:16 ('All scripture is inspired by God') could in fact equally be translated as 'God-breathed.' (see also *illumination*)

Liberal

Anyone less conservative in their interpretations than you are is a liberal. (see also *fundamentalist*)

Perspiration

After considering the God-breathed aspect of Scripture (see *inspiration*), many find that the rest of interpretation becomes sheer hard work. The technical term for this is *perspiration*.

Proof Texting

Using a Bible verse or passage out of context to provide a handy 'proof' of whatever point you were trying to make, regardless of what the Bible verse you used is actually about. Proof texting is extremely popular because it is much easier than interpreting the Bible properly.

Typology

(1) The view that Old Testament things or events 'stand for' later things or events and reveal truths about them (or 'prefigure' them) ahead of time. Paul, for instance, interprets the rock in the wilderness as Christ (1 Corinthians 10:4), and sees an old law about muzzling the ox as a principle relevant to the question of whether apostles should be paid for their work (1 Corinthians 9:9), which perhaps suggests that he had an interesting self-image.
(2) The study of which fonts the Bible was produced in.

Weather

When Ezra read from the book of the law in Ezra 10:9, the two things which distressed the crowds were (a) the realisation that they had sinned against God and (b) the heavy rain. The role of the weather in our understanding of the Bible remains a vastly under-explored subject.

Zwingli

A Swiss Reformer, not known especially for his ideas on hermeneutics, but whose name somehow always seems to be the last word on any subject.

FURTHER READING

Find out here how to spend the rest of your life reading about biblical interpretation: ideal for those who hope to avoid ever actually having to do any of it.

The problem for any book on biblical interpretation is how to spend time both clarifying and interpreting the biblical text as well as explaining why and how the various hermeneutical approaches work. Here, of course, we have done nothing but skim the surface of these issues, trying to pack in as many examples as possible while also showing that a lot of the jargon and concepts are nothing to be afraid of. But if you want to get down to some serious interpretation, where do you go next?

I have tried an approach to hermeneutics which works from interpreting specific biblical passages out towards thinking about biblical interpretation in a theological way in:

Richard Briggs, *Reading the Bible Wisely*, SPCK, 2003.

For more on the question of how to read the Bible as a theological book about God and God's desires for how we live see:

N.T. Wright, *Scripture and the Authority of God*, SPCK, 2005.

A good basic book for taking you through the different approaches needed for the various biblical genres is:

Gordon D. Fee & Douglas Stuart, *How to Read the Bible for all its Worth*, Zondervan, third edition, Zondervan, 2003.

There is a recent series of 'Exploring' study books which give you a very well organised survey of all the OT and NT books and introduce you to the kinds of questions they raise. They are designed as 'self-study' books with panels, charts and questions for further reflection, and they do an excellent job of guiding you into an understanding of what is in the Bible:

The four volumes of *Exploring the Old Testament* (SPCK) are:

Vol 1 – *The Pentateuch* – G. Wenham (2003)
Vol 2 – *History* – G. McConville & P. Satterthwaite (forthcoming)
Vol 3 – *The Psalms and Wisdom Literature* – E. Lucas (2003)
Vol 4 — *Prophets* – G. McConville (2002)

The two volumes of *Exploring the New Testament* (SPCK) are:

Vol 1 – *Introducing the Gospels and Acts* – D. Wenham & S. Walton (2001)
Vol 2 – *The Letters and Revelation* – I. H. Marshall, S. Travis & I. Paul (2002)

A slightly more demanding book which combines this kind of survey with more theoretical essays about interpretation is:

John Barton (ed), *The Cambridge Companion to Biblical Interpretation*, Cambridge, 1998.

Finally, for the more adventurous reader, a wonderful book on how to approach the biblical text with hermeneutical sensitivity, working with the test case of the Magi story in Matthew 2, is:

Mark Allan Powell, *Chasing the Eastern Star: Adventures in Biblical Reader-Response Criticism*, Westminster/John Knox Press, 2001.